Cake Decorating
for Everyone

Margie Smuts · Kinnie Human

Cake Decorating for Everyone

Human & Rousseau
Cape Town   Pretoria

The publication of this book at a reasonable price has been made possible by contributions from Hulett Refineries Limited and the Woolcraft & Hobby Shop.

The publisher would like to express thanks to Collectors Corner who kindly lent the accessories used in Photographs 17, 18 and 19.

Copyright © 1988 by Margie Smuts and Kinnie Human
First published in 1988 by Human & Rousseau (Pty) Ltd
State House, 3-9 Rose Street, Cape Town
Atrium Building, 60 Glenwood Road, Pretoria
Photography by Nico Oelofse and Annette Jahnel (pp. 97, 98 and 99)
Illustrations by Corrine Hoffman and Debbie Odendaal
Typography by Etienne van Duyker and Wiekie Theron
Cover design by Etienne van Duyker
Cover photograph by Annette Jahnel
Typeset in 11 on 12 pt Plantin Roman by Studiographix, Cape Town
Colour separations by Unifoto, Cape Town
Printed and bound by Printpak Books, Dacres Avenue, Epping

ISBN 0 7981 2310 9

Acknowledgements

I would firstly like to thank our Heavenly Father for granting me this talent and the privilege of sharing it with others, which in turn has provided me with an opportunity to serve Him. I would also like to express my thanks to my co-author Kinnie Human, the publisher, photographers, printers and everyone involved with the book; to Kate Venter, a real friend in need who helped to cover cakes when my strength failed me and who made flowers on flower nails as well as some of the cakes; to my daughter, Eulogia Murray, who found the time to lend a hand despite her full programme; to Dora van Heerden, Frances Bell and Mary Lake who each decorated a cake; and last but not least, to my husband who encouraged me over the years and never complained when my hobby consumed all of my attention.

MARGIE SMUTS

All my thanks to our Heavenly Father for helping me to achieve what I did with the talent He gave me. My thanks also to Margie Smuts, my co-author and founder of the South African Cake Decorators' Guild, for her inspiration; to the publisher, photographers and printers; to my daughters, Hester and Lona, as well as Fanie Strümpfer, who in the midst of studying and with little available time could still see their way clear to do my drawings; to Gwynn Müller, my most loyal friend, who helped with some of the cakes; and to my husband for his patience, sacrifices and encouragement.

KINNIE HUMAN

The authors would also like to thank Hulett Refineries Limited and the Woolcraft & Hobby Shop for their generous contributions.

Foreword

In recent years many good books on cake decorating have been written, each one highlighting aspects hitherto neglected.

Margie Smuts and Kinnie Human have now co-authored a book which touches on most aspects of the craft. It is an invaluable guide for the beginner, for whom the book is really intended, and the clear illustrations and concise instructions will ensure its place on every cake decorator's shelf.

Both authors have taught cake decorating in America and have also demonstrated at the International Cake Decorating Convention.

Margie Smuts has written books on a variety of subjects, including cake decorating. She is the founder of the South African Cake Decorators' Guild and with her great love for the craft and her dedication to promoting it, she has watched the Guild grow enormously since its inception only ten years ago.

Kinnie Human has also taught in Australia and is well equipped to write on the Australian technique of floodwork. A founder member of the Guild, she has freely shared her talents with fellow cake decorators over the past years, and her ideas have now been included in this book.

As one of the aims of the Guild is to share knowledge amongst members, various others have also contributed to the final product, thereby demonstrating this aim in a practical way. It gives me great pleasure to commend this book.

EUNICE BORCHERS
National PRO of the SA Cake Decorators' Guild

Contents

Introduction

Cake decorating, like all creative arts, is a source of pleasure to both the creator and appreciative audience. Although cake decorating is an established art form, there have been many significant changes in the field over the past few years. Not only has the quality of the decorations improved tremendously, the techniques have also been refined to a large extent. This by no means implies that all the proven methods should summarily be thrown overboard. They still serve as a source of inspiration for the cake decorator in the same way as the old masters have set a standard for today's artists. To master the techniques for the older types of decoration will always remain a challenge; in fact, many of the proven techniques form the basis of modern cake decorating.

There is a marked difference between commercial cake decorating (as done by bakers) and decorating for fun or for shows. In mass production, the time and money spent must always be taken into account. A home decorator who does it as a pastime, usually spares no expense or trouble in order to perfect her creation. Cake decorating can become a lucrative hobby or home industry as long as the profit motive does not overrule the artistry.

An artistic ability alone will not enable one to become a competent cake decorator. As is the case with any form of art, one first has to master certain basic techniques and skills, obtain the correct recipes and practise sufficiently. It is also important that one should always be critical of one's own creations and should be receptive to constructive criticism, especially when it comes from those at home. On the other hand, do not become despondent if your first attempts are not first-prize winners! Patience and perseverance have more often than not been the secret of success of many an average cake decorator.

It should be stressed that while this book supplies detailed instructions on how each type of decoration should be done, your own touch will determine the final result. Each creation should bear the stamp of its creator or it simply becomes yet another copy. Therefore, once you have mastered the techniques, do not be afraid to try your hand at original creations.

Because one learns so much from others, we would like to encourage you to join your nearest branch of the South African Cake Decorators' Guild. If there is no branch in your vicinity, join the Guild as a postal member to ensure that you are always kept up to date with any new developments in the field. The Guild's head office is in Johannesburg. The address is P.O. Box 96186, Brixton 2019, South Africa.

Cake decorating covers a wide spectrum of techniques, and book stores are filled with books attempting to cover the entire field. As a result the stress has fallen mainly on advanced cake decorating and sugarcraft, while in many instances the details of each technique have been neglected. This book is especially intended for people who have never had the opportunity to follow a course in this art form but would like to be able to decorate a cake attractively for the enjoyment of friends or family. If you fall into this category, we hope this book will inspire you to persevere and, if possible, enrol for a course with someone who holds the teaching certificate from the South African Cake Decorators' Guild. Once you have mastered the basic techniques described in this book, you will have a sound foundation on which to build.

Finally, we hope that this book will open up an entirely new field of experience – the sheer joy of being creative.

MARGIE SMUTS AND KINNIE HUMAN

CHAPTER 1

Some choice cake recipes

Even the most attractively decorated cake will be a disappointment if the cake itself is not successful or does not taste as good as it should. We have supplied a few proven cake recipes. For the best results we recommend the use of Huletts brown and castor sugar.

Sponge cake

Ingredients
375 g flour
25 ml baking powder
2 ml salt
8 eggs
450 g castor sugar
flavouring
300 ml milk (or half water)
62,5 ml cooking oil

Method
Sift the flour, baking powder and salt together. Beat the eggs well. Add the sugar and beat until the sugar has completely dissolved. The mixture should be light and smooth. Add flavouring to taste.

Bring the milk (or milk and water) and oil to the boil. Add it *very slowly* to the egg and sugar mixture while beating constantly. Fold in the sifted flour mixture (in two parts) by setting the mixer at a very slow speed after each addition and then beating it very fast for *5 seconds* only.

Note: Once the sifted flour and baking powder have been added, take care not to over-beat the mixture; just ensure that there are no lumps of flour left.

Bake for 25-40 minutes at 180 °C, depending on the depth of the tin. Three layer cakes in 230 mm x 75 mm tins should be baked for 25 minutes.

This mixture is used mostly for children's cakes such as the train cake or cut-up cakes, which explains the varying baking times. Do not spray or butter the cake tins: rather line the base with a piece of waxed paper cut to size. This will ensure that the sides of the cake remain neatly against the sides of the tin instead of curling inwards. Cut loose carefully – do not try to cut the cake loose in one cutting motion. This will only damage the sides.

Chocolate sponge cake

Substitute cocoa for 125 ml of the flour in the previous recipe. The method remains the same.

Five-egg mixture for a smaller cake

Ingredients
250 g flour
17 ml baking powder
1 ml salt
200 ml milk
42 ml cooking oil
5 eggs
300 g castor sugar
flavouring

Method
Follow the same method as for the sponge cake. Bake layer cakes in two 230 mm x 75 mm cake tins at 180 °C for 25 minutes.

For a chocolate cake, substitute cocoa for 80 ml flour.

Chocolate cake for the microwave oven

Ingredients
4 eggs
437 ml castor sugar
500 ml flour
80 ml cocoa
1 ml salt
15 ml baking powder
250 ml water
80 g butter or margarine

Method
Beat the eggs well. Add sugar *gradually* and beat well. Sift the flour, cocoa and salt together and fold into the egg mixture. Sprinkle baking powder over the mixture. *Do not stir.*

Boil the water and butter for 1 minute, pour over the mixture and *fold* in. Quickly pour into two buttered 210 mm x 75 mm glass or plastic containers. Place the "tins" on egg containers. Bake *each cake* for 2 minutes at MEDIUM HIGH, followed by 3½ minutes at HIGH.

Cherry and sultana cake

Ingredients
300 g margarine
350 g castor sugar
6 eggs
5 ml lemon essence
575 g flour
20 ml baking powder
2 ml salt
300 ml milk
200 g sultanas
150 g cherries (the fruit can be left out in a child's
  cake)

Method
Cream the margarine and sugar. Add the eggs one by
one, stirring well after each addition. Add a little flour
after the third egg to prevent the mixture curdling. Add
the flavouring.

  Sift the flour, baking powder and salt together. Add
alternately with the milk to the egg mixture. Finally add
the fruit.

  Neatly line a 230 mm x 75 mm tin with two layers of
brown paper and then a layer of buttered greaseproof
paper. Pour the mixture into the tin and bake approximately ¾-1 hour (depending on the size of the tin)
at 180 °C.

Light fruitcake

Ingredients
375 g flour
7 ml baking powder
2 ml salt
250 g butter
250 g castor sugar
6 eggs
500 g mixed fruit
250 g cherries, cut in half
55 g nuts, chopped
100 ml brandy
5 ml lemon essence

Method
Sift the dry ingredients together. Cream the butter and
add the sugar gradually. Beat the mixture well after
each addition. Add the eggs one by one. Add a little flour
after the third egg to prevent the mixture curdling. Add
the fruit, cherries and nuts. Fold in the dry ingredients
and add the brandy and lemon essence. Mix.

  Neatly line a 230 mm x 75 mm tin with a few layers of
brown paper and a layer of buttered greaseproof paper.

  Bake for 2-2½ hours at 140-180 °C.

Dark fruitcake

Ingredients
1 kg mixed fruit (currants, sultanas and raisins)
250 g dates, shredded
350 g castor sugar
7 ml bicarbonate of soda
250 g butter or margarine
375 ml sweet wine
200 g cherries, cut in half
60 g mixed peel
175 ml brandy
4 eggs
575 g flour
15 ml baking powder
10 ml mixed spice
20 ml cocoa
10 ml ground ginger
5 ml nutmeg
2 ml salt
flavouring to taste

Method
Wash the mixed fruit well and leave to dry. Place the
fruit, dates, sugar, bicarbonate of soda and butter in a
heavy-bottomed saucepan and pour the sweet wine
over. Cover and boil for 5 minutes. Allow the mixture to
cool and add the cherries, mixed peel and brandy. Beat
the eggs well, add to the mixture and blend well.

  Sift the flour, baking powder, mixed spice, cocoa,
ginger, salt and nutmeg together. Add to the fruit mixture and blend well. Add flavouring.

  Neatly line a 250 mm x 75 mm tin with a few layers of
brown paper and then a layer of buttered greaseproof
paper. Bake in a 120 °C oven for 1 hour and then for 4¼
hours at 110 °C. (These temperatures have been tested
at sea-level and will have to be adapted up country,
especially in high-lying areas.)

  This cake can be kept for a long period as it is baked
slowly and the fruit is cooked without burning.

Dark fruitcake for the microwave oven

Ingredients
750 g fruitcake mix
250 g dates, shredded
60 g glazed pineapple, cubed
100 g cherries, cut in half
250 g butter or margarine
180 ml water
200 ml brown sugar
5 ml bicarbonate of soda
100 g nuts, chopped
100 ml brandy

500 ml flour
5 ml baking powder
5 ml mixed spice
2 ml ground ginger
2 ml ground nutmeg
2 ml cinnamon
1 ml ground cloves
2 eggs, beaten

Method
Mix the fruitcake mix, dates, pineapple, cherries, butter, water, brown sugar and bicarbonate of soda in a heavy-bottomed saucepan. Boil for 7 minutes. Remove from heat and add the nuts and brandy. Blend well.

Sift flour, baking powder and spices together and add to the fruit mixture, alternately with the beaten egg. Mix thoroughly.

Line the base of a buttered 230 mm x 100 mm soufflé dish with paper towelling. (The paper towelling absorbs moisture, which prevents the bottom of the cake becoming soggy.) If using a square dish, protect the sides with aluminium foil. Pour the mixture into the dish and smooth the surface. Place it in the microwave oven on top of a rack or an upturned pudding-bowl and bake for 18-22 minutes at MEDIUM. *Leave in the dish for 5 minutes,* test to ensure that the cake is done and turn out on a rack covered with paper towelling. Sprinkle extra brandy over the bottom of the cake and turn the cake over as soon as it has been absorbed. Sprinkle some brandy over the top of the cake and cover with paper towelling. Allow the cake to cool before wrapping it in aluminium foil to ripen. Sprinkle with a little brandy every two weeks.

The fruitcake mix can be replaced with glazed fruit such as watermelon, ginger or green figs as long as the fruit weighs 750 g.

CHAPTER 2

Various icings and their uses

To obtain the best results it is essential that you use the best quality ingredients. We confidently recommend Huletts sugar, icing sugar, castor sugar and marzipan.

All icing sugar contains small quantities of cornflour to prevent lumps forming. Determine the quantity of cornflour in icing sugar by adding 5 ml icing sugar to 250 ml water. Stir and leave for a while. The slight sediment at the bottom of the glass will indicate the amount of cornflour. It is important that the amount of cornflour be kept to a minimum in very delicate decorations as well as to ensure the fine texture characteristic of royal icing. Experience has taught us that Huletts icing sugar best complies with this prerequisite. The packaging also prevents lumps forming. This icing sugar is therefore recommended by the South African Cake Decorators' Guild.

1. Decoration with dry icing sugar

If you have baked a sponge cake for morning tea and there is no time to mix an icing, you can still decorate your cake effortlessly and attractively by using dry icing sugar and a sieve. Cut a piece of paper the size of the cake's surface. Fold the paper into six or eight sections and cut out a design (dolls, flowers or symmetrical designs). Iron the paper flat, place it on the cake and, using a fine sieve, evenly sift the icing sugar over the cake. Carefully lift the design from the cake with a quick upward movement and voilá! you have an instant iced cake. An attractive paper doily with a suitably open design can also be used.

2. Sugar ornaments

Sugar ornaments, made from moist castor sugar formed in plastic moulds, are ideal for decorating children's cakes and Christmas cakes.

Ingredients
500 ml castor sugar
20 ml water or egg white

Method
Place the castor sugar in a bowl and add the water. Mix by hand until the mixture has the texture of moist sea sand. Cover with a damp cloth until needed.

Test the texture by squeezing a little of the mixture in your hand. If it leaves clear fingermarks, it is ready for use. If the mixture is too dry and tends to crumble, add a little water. If it is too moist and sticks to the fingers, add a little extra castor sugar.

To colour the mixture, add the colouring to the water. The dry ornaments can be finished with a little edible glitter (see following recipe).

3. Edible glitter

Ingredients
12,5 ml gum arabic (obtainable from your chemist)
12,5 ml water

Method
Mix the ingredients until all the gum has dissolved. Add colouring if desired.

Paint a thin layer of the mixture (like varnish) on a heat-resistant glass or stainless steel surface and bake it in a very slow oven at about 110 °C. Carefully remove the mixture from the oven as soon as it begins to crack and break, and scrape it from the surface. If it is not fine enough, rub it through a sieve. Repeat until the mixture is finished. Edible glitter keeps for years if put into a sealed container.

4. Piping gel

This versatile icing can be bought ready-made in a wide variety of colours or in a neutral colour. It is shiny and therefore perfect for brightening up any decoration (see Photographs 17 and 18 on pp. 97 and 98). Because it is transparent, it can be used to add shine to a window. It is especially suitable for decorating cupcakes or children's cakes. When painting on rice paper, it is essential that the rice paper first be painted with this gel to prevent the edges curling over.

5. Almond paste or marzipan

It is essential to cover a fruitcake with marzipan before covering it with fondant or royal icing. It not only enhances the flavour of the cake, but also protects the cake and prevents grease stains seeping through to the final covering and spoiling the appearance of the cake. It is an excellent base for the final covering of the cake, prevents crumbs mixing with the covering (in the case of royal icing) and improves the overall appearance of the cake. Ready-made marzipan is not made from real almonds; for the gourmet we therefore provide the following recipe:

Ingredients
1 egg or 2 egg yolks
250 g finely ground almonds
375 g icing sugar
125 g castor sugar
12,5 ml brandy
5 ml almond or vanilla essence

Method
Add the egg to the ground almonds and mix well. Add the icing sugar and castor sugar a spoonful at a time and blend thoroughly. Add the brandy and flavouring.

Knead the paste by hand when it becomes too stiff to stir with a wooden spoon. Shape into a stiff ball, sprinkle icing sugar in the bowl or on a wooden board and knead thoroughly. The paste should be stiff but not too dry. It should resemble smooth bread dough and be easy to roll out without cracking or sticking to the rolling-pin.

Ready-made marzipan should also be kneaded thoroughly before being rolled out. If it is too dry a little egg yolk can be added, and if it is too soft a little icing sugar will do the trick. Ensure, however, that any additions are thoroughly kneaded.

A simnel cake is delicious when covered with almond paste or marzipan (see Method 3 p. 36).

MARZIPAN FOR MODELLING
Ingredients
375 g marzipan
250 g icing sugar
10 ml gelatine
10 ml cold water
10 ml boiling water
1 egg white

Method
Cover the ready-made marzipan with foil (or waxed paper in the case of a microwave oven) and place in the oven to warm. Grease a bowl with vegetable fat and warm the icing sugar in a bowl over boiling water. Moisten the gelatine with cold water, then add the boiling water. Stand in a bowl of warm water until melted. Make a well in the icing sugar, pour the gelatine and the egg white into the well and mix thoroughly. Add the marzipan. Coat your hands well with vegetable fat and knead thoroughly.

If the icing is too soft for use, cover with aluminium foil and place it in the refrigerator until stiff, or add a little extra icing sugar. Take care not to warm the icing sugar too much before use as heat will reduce the gelatine's elasticity.

This paste is used to model flowers, elves, etc.

ALTERNATIVE RECIPE FOR MARZIPAN MODELLING
Mix 250 g marzipan with 25 ml fondant icing or with 12,5 ml fondant icing and 12,5 ml gum paste. If too stiff and brittle, add 12,5 ml brandy. Knead well and do not colour the marzipan.

6. Glacé icing

This easy icing is used only to cover cakes and not to decorate them. Although there are many variations, they are all basically the same. We will provide the basic recipe first, followed by a few variations. It is a soft, satiny mixture which runs evenly and quickly forms a thin crust. It is especially suitable for sponge cakes and *petits fours*. If you are in a hurry it is a real timesaver as it can be made within minutes. It is also economical and enhances the flavour of the cake.

Ingredients
250 ml icing sugar
13 ml warm water
colouring
flavouring

(The quantities will be determined by the way in which the icing is to be used.)

Method
Sift the icing sugar well. Add the warm water gradually and stir well. Add the colouring and flavouring. The texture should resemble that of thick cream. If it is too runny it will run off the cake too quickly, and if it is too thick it will not run evenly. (The next chapter explains in detail how to use this icing.)

For the technique of mixing and applying the glacé icing, see Photographs 1a and b.

Photograph 1a

Photograph 1b

Variations

• *Chocolate glacé icing*
Break a few squares of chocolate into a double boiler and heat with 12,5 ml milk and 12,5 ml water. When the chocolate has melted, add 50 ml icing sugar and mix well. Increase the quantities as necessary.

• *Mocha glacé icing*
Sift 12,5 ml cocoa and 375 ml icing sugar together. Add hot, strong coffee and mix to a thick cream. Add approximately 5 ml melted butter to enhance the flavour. Instead of coffee, 5 ml coffee extract or powder can be sifted with the dry ingredients and mixed with hot water only. The cocoa can also be left out for a coffee icing.

• *Lemon or orange glacé icing*
Mix the icing sugar with lemon or orange juice.

• *Spicy glacé icing*
Mix 2 ml mixed spice, 2 ml nutmeg and 2 ml ground cinnamon with the icing sugar before adding the water.

7. American frosting or seven-minute frosting

Ingredients
375 ml sugar
125 ml cold water
pinch of cream of tartar
pinch of salt
2 egg whites
5 ml flavouring

Method
Place the sugar and water in the top of a double boiler with boiling water. Add the cream of tartar, egg white and flavouring. Beat, using an electric mixer, for approximately 7 minutes at high speed or until the mixture forms peaks when lifting the mixer. Remove from the heat and beat some more. Spread evenly over the cake or make small peaks for decoration.

Variations

• Add 12,5 ml cocoa to the mixture once it reaches a temperature of 120 °C.
• Use honey instead of sugar. It is not as sweet and enhances the flavour.
• Instead of sugar, use two squares of melted chocolate, 50 ml honey and 250 g icing sugar and replace 125 ml cold water with 25 ml warm water. The icing will be slightly more runny and should be used immediately.

8. Butter icing

Butter icing is used as a covering for soft cakes or as a filling for layer cakes. It is also suitable for decorating cakes. Decorations in butter icing can be used in royal icing on fruitcakes, but not vice versa. Modelled flowers used on a fruitcake are not suitable for a cake covered with butter icing. The decoration on a soft cake covered in butter icing should not be too time-consuming as these cakes are usually not kept for a long period.

Ingredients
125 g butter or margarine
500 g icing sugar

a few drops lemon juice, warm milk, water or fruit juice
(to dilute the icing if necessary)
flavouring
colouring

Method
Beat the shortening, using a wooden spoon, until soft and creamy. Sift the icing sugar and add a spoonful at a time to the shortening, mixing thoroughly. If the mixture is too stiff, dilute with a little lemon juice or warm milk. Add flavouring and beat continuously until the mixture has the texture of well beaten, thick cream. (The spoon should remain upright in the mixture.) Carefully add the desired colouring – a too delicate colour can always be made darker, but a dark colour cannot easily be made lighter.

Variations

• Many variations are possible with the addition of different flavourings and ingredients. Chocolate or coffee icing is made by adding cocoa or strong coffee instead of milk. Mocha icing is made by adding both coffee and cocoa.

9. Royal icing

This icing was once used to cover fruitcakes (it is still used as covering in England) but because it is so hard a softer icing is used for covering cakes in South Africa. However, it still remains the only icing used for decorations on fruitcakes. Delicate lace is also made from royal icing.

Although the main ingredients are egg white and icing sugar, there are quite a few factors which will determine the quality of the texture, of which the method of mixing is definitely the most important.

Ingredients
3 egg whites
450 g icing sugar, sifted (the quantity will depend largely on the size of the eggs)
5 ml rose water
5 ml tartaric acid (some people use acetic acid, but since it is poisonous we prefer to use tartaric acid)
a few drops of blue colouring if a pure white icing is required

Method
Beat the egg whites well (not too dry) and add the sifted icing sugar a spoonful at a time, beating after each addition. The final texture will depend on how well the icing sugar was beaten every time. Preferably this icing should be beaten by hand, using a wooden spoon; if using an electric mixer, set it at the slowest speed to ensure that as little air as possible is beaten into the mixture.

The icing has the required texture if it forms a peak when a knife is drawn through the mixture, lifted and turned (see Photograph 2). Add the flavouring and tartaric acid. Carefully add colouring if desired. For a white icing, add a few drops of blue colouring.

Cover the icing with a damp cloth or clingwrap. Before using the icing, remove any air-bubbles by working it through with a knife.

ROYAL ICING USED WITH FINE TUBES NOS 1, 0 AND 00
Ordinary royal icing tends to block the small openings of these tubes which are normally used for delicate filigree.

The following method for sifting and mixing has been

Photograph 2

tried and tested, and although it might seem a bit tedious the result is worthwhile. It is preferable not to mix large quantities at a time as tiny, hard lumps might form if it is left to stand.

Ingredients
10 ml egg white, beaten and at room temperature
icing sugar, finely sifted

For the best results, use only the finest, top quality icing sugar. Huletts icing sugar meets these standards.

Requirements
a piece of finely woven material for sifting the sugar (Terylene is recommended; chiffon is too loosely woven while a stocking is too elastic)

a plastic bowl with a tight-fitting lid in which to sift the sugar

a glass or porcelain bowl or cup with a round base in which to mix the icing (do not use a plastic bowl as tiny bits of plastic chip off and end up in the icing during the process)

Method
Use only 5 ml egg white at a time for mixing. Have the icing bags and tubes ready beforehand in order to fill the bags immediately once the icing is prepared. This will prevent any dry bits of icing forming. It is preferable to use small plastic or greaseproof paper bags. A grease-proof paper bag covered with a plastic bag will also prevent the icing from drying out. Ensure that your equipment is spotlessly clean and free of any grease or dust – even the tiniest dust particle can block a tube. Wipe each piece of equipment or bowl thoroughly before use.

Place the piece of material over the plastic bowl to form a well (see Fig. 1). Put 5-6 ml icing sugar into the well and cover tightly with the lid. Sift the sugar by holding the bowl in one hand and shaking it firmly against the other hand. All the sugar should be sifted within 3 minutes. Transfer it to a clean bowl and cover with a piece of clingwrap. Shake any sugar still adhering to the material into another bowl (to avoid getting confused, use one which looks different from the bowl containing the sifted icing sugar).

After about 15 minutes you should have enough sifted sugar (100 ml) to use with 10 ml egg white.

Note: *Sifting the icing sugar is the most important step in the entire procedure!*

Break the egg white slightly and force it through a piece of material. Ensure that the white membrane in the egg white remains behind on the material. Place 10 ml egg white in the porcelain bowl or cup and beat slightly. Add the sifted icing sugar a teaspoonful at a time, mixing well after each addition. (Keep a damp cloth handy to wipe the sides of the bowl to prevent a hard crust forming.) Continue until the mixture forms a soft peak. If the peak collapses immediately the mixture is still too soft for a fine tube as any piping will thicken once it has passed through the tube. If the peak remains upright, the mixture is too stiff and a little extra egg white should be added to soften it.

As soon as the mixture has the correct consistency, the icing bags must be filled immediately and the tips of the tubes put into a wet sponge or cloth.

The following recipe (courtesy of Kate Venter) can also be used, especially for extension work with a No 0 tube:

± 200 g icing sugar
2,5 ml gum tragacanth or gum arabic
1 egg white, at room temperature
5 ml liquid glucose

Sift the gum arabic and the icing sugar together through the material. Proceed as described above. Finally, add the glucose. Alternatively, the gum arabic and icing sugar can be sifted together and kept in an airtight container. If you mix in 10 ml egg white at a time, you will only need to add a *tiny* drop of glucose.

10. Icing for floodwork

This is in fact diluted royal icing and is used to flood cake collars and all kinds of loose ornaments, figurines, etc. Royal icing can be diluted with water until it becomes runny, or the mixture can be runny from the outset, in which case it will not be necessary to add any water. To prevent air-bubbles forming, do not overbeat. Leave the prepared icing for a while to remove any air that may be trapped.

The consistency depends on what the icing is to be used for. It is usually tested by drawing a knife through the mixture. The mark left by the knife should gradually disappear and the surface should become smooth again. For ordinary collars and other "flat" floodwork this closing-up procedure should last about ten counts. For built-up and three-dimensional work the procedure will take longer, depending on the required result.

11. Fondant (as recommended by the South African Cake Decorators' Guild)

Ingredients
250 g liquid glucose (half a bottle)

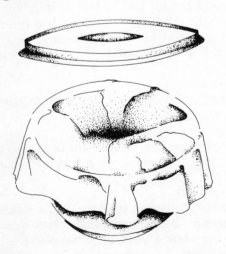

Fig. 1

10 ml gelatine
50 ml cold water
20 g white vegetable fat (Holsum)
1 kg icing sugar, sifted

Method
Leave the open bottle of glucose in warm water. Sift an additional 250 ml icing sugar in which eventually to roll the fondant. Soak the gelatine in the cold water and leave the container in boiling water until the gelatine has dissolved completely and is transparent. Melt the vegetable fat.

Make a well in the sifted icing sugar and add the gelatine, glucose and melted vegetable fat. Stir thoroughly and knead well on a surface on which the additional 250 ml icing sugar has been sprinkled. If the mixture becomes too stiff add a little egg white, and if it is too runny add a little more icing sugar until the texture is smooth and pliable.

12. Plastic icing (as approved by the South African Cake Decorators' Guild)

Ingredients
250 ml sugar
250 g liquid glucose (half a bottle)
125 ml water
10 ml gelatine
15 ml cold water
flavouring
colouring
20 g white vegetable fat (Holsum)
1 kg icing sugar

Method
Melt the sugar and glucose in the water. Ensure that the sugar has melted completely. Always keep the sides of the saucepan clean by wiping it with a clean, wet brush or a piece of wet cotton wool. Bring to the boil and cover with the lid for 1-2 minutes in order to steam-clean the sides of the saucepan.

Heat to 110 °C. This should take about 4 minutes. Do not stir while the mixture is boiling. Remove from the heat. Once the mixture stops bubbling, add the gelatine which has been soaking in 15 ml cold water. Add flavouring and/or colouring.

Sift the icing sugar on to a large even surface, make a well in the centre and pour the mixture into the well. Mix and knead until a smooth, pliable texture is obtained.

Roll out (Photograph 3) and cover the cake while the icing is still warm. This icing can be reheated in an oven at 110 °C.

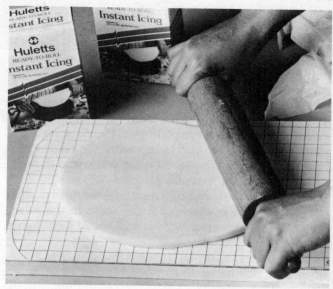

Photograph 3

You can buy ready-made fondant icings which save time and are delicious, especially if blended with a little flavouring. These icings should be well kneaded before use. (Coat your hands with vegetable fat before kneading.) The icing should be smooth and pliable. To test the pliability, form a roll of icing and fold it over. If it cracks, it should be kneaded a bit more.

13. Modelling paste

Although we will not be doing much modelling work in this book (it is advanced work and we would like to devote our attention to work for the beginner) we still feel this recipe for modelling paste could be useful.

Ingredients
15 ml gum tragacanth or the more economical CMC (Sodium Carboxy Methyl Cellulose), obtainable from your chemist
500 ml icing sugar, sifted
10 ml gelatine
15 ml cold water
10 ml liquid glucose (optional at sea level or in areas with a high humidity)
1 egg white, beaten
vegetable fat (Holsum)

Method
Sift the tragacanth and 250 ml of the icing sugar in a bowl. Soak the gelatine in the cold water and leave for about 5 minutes. Melt the gelatine (preferably in a small double boiler) over boiling water and immediately add the glucose. (The glucose will run off the spoon more

easily if the spoon is first dipped in boiling water.) When all the granules have disappeared, the gelatine is ready to be added to the following mixture which has been prepared beforehand.

Add the beaten egg white to the icing sugar and gum tragacanth. Mix thoroughly. Add the melted gelatine and glucose and mix well. Continue adding icing sugar and mixing thoroughly. It makes the mixing easier if you place the bowl over boiling water. As soon as the mixture becomes too stiff to mix with a wooden spoon, coat your hands with vegetable fat and knead the mixture until it is smooth and pliable.

Roll up the paste in clingwrap and store until needed. If well wrapped it will keep for months in the refrigerator. Remove every few days and knead thoroughly.

QUICK MODELLING PASTE
Instant modelling paste can be obtained by adding a little gum tragacanth (or CMC) and an egg white to the plastic icing and kneading it by hand (remember to coat your hands with vegetable fat). As it is inclined to become soft in warm, humid weather, this instant version is not recommended for flowers that have to last for any length of time.

14. Pastillage

Ingredients
2 ml liquid glucose
50 ml cold water
500 ml icing sugar, sifted
12,5 ml CMC or gum tragacanth
cornflour for rolling out pastillage

Method
Dissolve the glucose in 25 ml cold water. Mix the icing sugar and gum tragacanth, make a well in the mixture and add the liquid. Mix thoroughly. Sprinkle a little icing sugar on the working surface and pour the mixture on to it. Knead thoroughly. If it is too soft, incorporate more sugar until the mixture has the texture of Plasticine.

Sprinkle cornflour on the working surface and roll out into a thin layer: about 1,3 mm for cards and other decorations, but slightly thicker for plaques.

CHAPTER 3

Bags, bowls and other equipment

Although a resourceful and artistic cake decorator can cope without the correct equipment, it is preferable to acquire the correct, best quality tools. At present the Woolcraft & Hobby Shop in Pietermaritzburg is one of the largest suppliers of cake decorating equipment in South Africa.

It is also advisable to keep all your cake decorating equipment together and to use it only for this purpose. The plastic boxes used by fishermen are ideal for storing smaller pieces of equipment. Icing tubes are easily bent and should not be carelessly stored in a drawer or cardboard box. The brush and ruler used for cake decoration should always be spotlessly clean. We cannot stress enough how important it is that any tools used for cake decoration should always be perfectly clean and used only for their intended purpose. A cupboard for storing completed flowers or ornaments is also recommended.

The following is a list of the most important pieces of equipment used in this book.

1. MIXING BOWL. A suitable bowl – preferably not plastic as any greasiness in the bowl might end up in the mixture.

2. WOODEN SPOON. A wooden spoon used exclusively for cake decorating. If it is used for other purposes, greasiness might seep into the wood and spoil the texture of royal icing. Fine wooden splinters might chip off into the icing if the spoon has been used for scraping out saucepans or other bowls.

3. ICING TUBES. There are many types of tubes available and it would be impossible to mention all the numbers of the different trade names here. Accordingly, we've only supplied the details of those tubes used most frequently in this book.

Icing tubes can be divided into the following categories:

Writing tubes (Fig. 2)
These tubes are not used exclusively for writing. However, writing or lettering is seldom, if ever, piped with any other tube. The round opening at the tip of the tube increases in size as the numbers increase. Following are some trade names and their corresponding numbers:
Tala and Probus: 1, 2, 3
Bekenal: 00, 0, 1, 2, 3
Errington: 1, 2, 3
Wiltons: 1, 2, 3
Ateco: 1, 2, 3
Magic Tip: 1, 2, 3

Ribbon tubes (Fig. 3)
These tubes with their even or evenly serrated tips are used to pipe ribbons and bows. We recommend the following numbers:
Tala and Probus: 9, 30, 34, 35
Wiltons: 46, 47
Ateco: 46, 48
Magic Tip: 46, 47

Star tubes (Fig. 4)
These tubes have star-tipped openings and are used to pipe stars, star and reverse scrolls, ropes, basket weave, shell and other borders (see p. 37). It is useful to have the following numbers:
Tala and Probus: 5, 6, 7, 8, 13
Errington: 5, 13
Wiltons: 28, 35
Ateco: 13, 14, 15, 16
Magic Tip: 27, 30

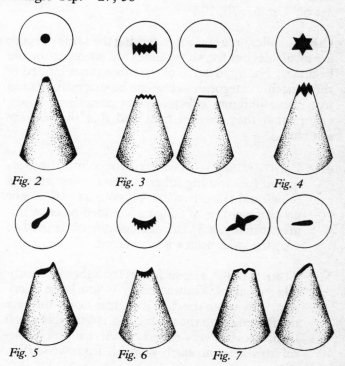

Fig. 2   Fig. 3   Fig. 4

Fig. 5   Fig. 6   Fig. 7

Petal tubes (Fig. 5)

These tubes are cut at an angle. The opening is wide at one end and narrow at the other end of the tip. The openings of some tubes are slightly curved. Petal tubes are available in different sizes and are used mainly for piping tube flowers on flower nails (see p. 48). The following are popular numbers:

Tala and Probus: 11, 18, 36, 42
Errington: 68, 71, 72 and especially 73b
Wiltons: 101, 102, 104
Ateco: 59s, 60, 61, 101
Magic Tip: 101, 101s, 104

Shell tubes (Fig. 6)

These tubes have serrated curves at one end and even-edged curves at the other. They are mostly used to pipe shell borders, although a star tube is also suitable for this purpose. The following numbers are useful:

Tala and Probus: 12
Errington: 172 (large)
Wiltons: 98
Ateco: 98
Magic Tip: 98

Leaf tubes (Fig. 7)

Two different types of tube can be used to pipe leaves. Both can also be used to pipe frills (see p. 41). The numbers for the two recommended tubes are:

Tala and Probus: 10, 11, 17, 38
Errington: 67, 68
Wiltons: 69, 102
Ateco: 67, 70, 102
Magic Tip: 67, 70, 102

Other smaller or larger tubes serving the same purpose are available, but the above tubes are adequate for the beginner. The application of the tubes is not limited to their specific categories – they can be successfully used to achieve different effects. When purchasing tubes, ensure that they are not bent and that the tips are not closed.

4.   PAINTBRUSHES.   A watercolour paintbrush is required for cleaning tubes. A few smaller brushes (Nos 0 and 1) are used to apply colour to a flower or an ornament or to adjust a lopsided piece of filigree. Finally, a 3 cm wide paintbrush is used to coat the cake before it is covered.

5.   TURNTABLE.   The surface of the light metal turntable available commercially is too large. Consequently when the cake is slightly heavy the base turns along with the top section. Adjustable metal turntables are very expensive. An extremely useful turntable can easily be made from wood (Fig.

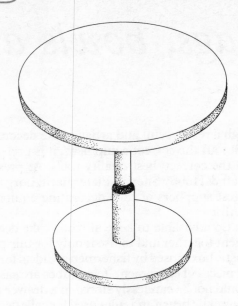

Fig. 8

8). The top section could be made of glass to facilitate cleaning and prevent warping. When you have the glass cut, have a hole cut in the centre so that the screw can be screwed in flush with the glass. Place a piece of felt underneath the glass and do not screw in too tightly.

6.   FLOWER NAILS.   There are many different sizes but if they are unobtainable you can easily make them yourself from the top of a cooldrink bottle. Simply solder a nail to the inside (Fig. 9).

7.   KNIVES, SCISSORS AND TWEEZERS.   A knife with a straight edge and a smaller bent spatula for picking up petals are essential. A small, extremely

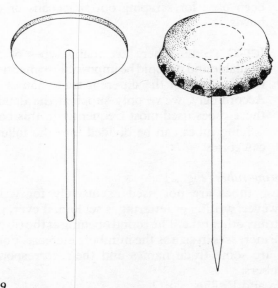

Fig. 9

sharp knife is also useful. You will need a large pair of scissors for cutting out patterns and a small pair of nail scissors when modelling small flowers. Tweezers are useful for positioning delicate stamens.

8.   ICING BAGS.   It is easy and convenient to make icing bags from greaseproof paper (not waxed paper) preferably the kind bought at cake decorating shops. If that is unobtainable, the kind bought in rolls at supermarkets will do. Ordinary greaseproof paper is not very sturdy and it is therefore suggested that you make your bag from two layers of paper.

There are two methods for folding an icing bag. Try both and see which suits you better. Do not give up if you have difficulty in folding the bag the first time. Follow the instructions carefully and try again until you get it right. The bag should be very sturdy and the bottom end should have a sharp point.

Bag no. 1 (Fig. 10).   Take a triangular piece of paper with corners A, B and C. Fold into a cornet with the sharp point, X, in the centre of the long side of the triangle. Corners A, B and C should coincide as far as possible at the top. Fold the corners over a few times to reinforce the bag. Cut a piece off the point so that the icing tube will fit in it snugly. You are now ready to begin.

Bag no. 2 (Fig. 11).   Take a rectangular piece of paper,

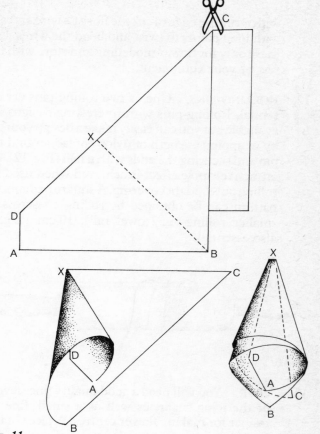

Fig. 11

350 mm x 230 mm, and fold it as illustrated. Cut it along the folded edge. Fold the paper so that point X is situated below B on the line CD. The line BX should be perpendicular to CD. Keeping your thumb at X, fold A to B to form a sharp point at X. Note that A does not match B and that B will be perpendicular to D. Bring C around the cone to B and ensure that the point (X) remains sharp. Tighten the bag, fold the corners over twice or secure them with a pin until the bag has been filled with icing. Cut the bottom point of the bag so that the tube will fit snugly when you fill the bag with icing.

9.   FLOWER CONTAINERS.   These are used for drying the petals of modelled flowers. Muffin tins or the material used for packing apples is suitable for this purpose. The latter can be cut into separate containers. Plastic ice trays, egg containers or a piece of foam rubber with hollows are all suitable for storing small petals.

10.   FLORIST'S WIRE.   Use Nos 22, 24, 26 and 0,3 mm thick florist's wire, green florist's adhesive tape and fuse wire to fasten stamens.

11.   PLIERS.   You will need two pairs of pliers: one

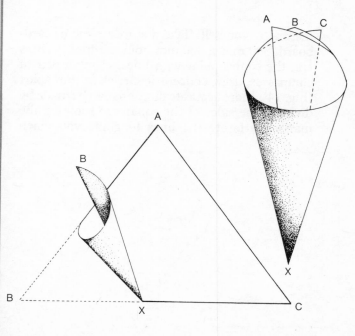

Fig. 10

with a cutting edge to cut the florist's wire and one with long points to twist and bend the wires. Use these only for flower modelling and store with the rest of your equipment.

12. ROLLING-PINS.   One or two rolling-pins are essential. Rolling-pins with interesting designs are available but you can easily make a design yourself by wrapping a length of nylon thread around the pin and securing the ends with a nail (Fig. 12). An attractive ripple effect is achieved when used for rolling out fondant covering. A square or diamond pattern can be obtained by rolling crisscross. A smaller rolling-pin (towel rail), 10 cm long, is also essential.

Fig. 12

13. SIEVE.   You will need a good quality fine sieve to sift the icing sugar, as well as a small, fine tea strainer for making flower centres. A piece of fine plastic gauze can be used instead of a sieve.

14. STAMENS.   These are obtainable from a florist or a cake decorating shop (the Woolcraft & Hobby Shop stocks a wide selection). You can make them yourself by using nylon thread or pale yellow or rose-coloured thread. A piece of unravelled nylon rope will also do the trick.

15. LEAF AND PETAL CUTTERS.   There is a wide variety of cutters for all types of flowers available commercially. Alternatively, you can draw designs on thin pieces of cardboard yourself and cut them out.

16. LARGE BEADS, MARBLES OR TABLE TENNIS BALLS.   Petals are dried over these.

17. A THICK PIECE OF GLASS OR A PLASTIC TABLE-MAT.   The glass or mat is used as a modelling surface. Small flowers can be modelled on a piece of foam rubber.

18. COTTON WOOL.   Always keep cotton wool handy when modelling flowers.

19. NYLON OR TERYLENE.   Keep a piece of nylon or Terylene handy when doing very delicate lace work. This is used with a plastic container with a tightly fitting lid and two small containers (see p. 17).

20. TOOLS FOR MODELLING.   The market is inundated with a wide variety of modelling tools. The beginner, however, only needs a few multi-purpose pieces. In *Sugarcraft,* the quarterly magazine of the South African Cake Decorators' Guild, new equipment is always being advertised. The Woolcraft & Hobby Shop in Pietermaritzburg is the largest stockist and it could be useful to browse through its catalogue. Here is an example of the kind of tools required by the beginner (Fig. 13). It is always worthwhile to acquire the correct tools.

21. PATTERN MARKERS.   You can make this useful piece of equipment, which is also available com-

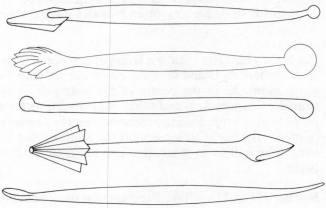

Fig. 13

mercially, yourself. Take a sturdy piece of cardboard, 300 mm x 300 mm, join the four corners and the centre point with lines. Using a pair of compasses, draw concentric circles 25 mm apart (Fig. 14). More accurate divisions can be made by dividing the sides of the square and joining the marks. Perforate the lines to guide you when

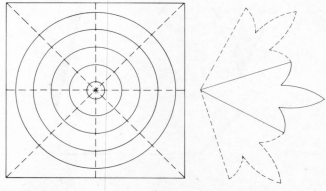

Fig. 14

dividing a cake for a pattern. Any pattern can be made with the use of these divisions. However, it is better first to trace the pattern on paper, cut it out and then carefully mark it on the cake.

22. CRIMPERS. A cake can be beautifully decorated with the clever use of these instruments. Interesting patterns are provided in the chapter on crimping (see p. 61). A wide variety of crimpers is available commercially and the Woolcraft & Hobby Shop has an excellent selection. They are also the manufacturers of the Kinnie crimpers. Here are a few examples some of which can be made by any handy toolmaker (Fig. 15).

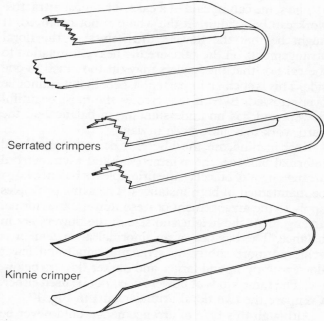

Serrated crimpers

Kinnie crimper

Fig. 15

General hints

At the risk of repetition, here are a few general hints which you should be aware of in advance.

1. Eggs
If a recipe calls for egg whites, it is preferable not to use fresh eggs – they should be at least seven days old. This advice applies especially to those who have access to farm-fresh eggs – shop-bought eggs have often been on the shelf for at least a week. Never use frozen egg whites – it will spoil the texture of the icing.

2. Climatic conditions
If you live in a very humid area, for example near the sea, you will find that the icing often does not harden or that a beautifully decorated cake will suddenly spoil because the icing has softened. Modelling and delicate lace work are also affected by high humidity. In these areas it is advisable to have a heater on in the room (even though it might be boiling hot!). Store the cake in an airtight cupboard with a burning electric light bulb. Enthusiasts who stay in humid areas are advised to have a special cupboard made with a few holes in the door for air circulation and fitted with a burning electric bulb inside. Silica gel (light pink crystals obtainable from your chemist) also helps to absorb any moisture. If you want to preserve one cake only and you do not have the proper facilities, put some of the crystals in the container with the cake. If the crystals turn blue, put them in a slow oven to dry them out. They will return to their former light pink colour. The crystals are re-usable.

3. Ants
These little pests are the cake decorator's biggest nightmare. However, they can be kept at bay if you take the necessary precautions. Sprinkle baby powder or kitchen scouring powder around the cake. If you are plagued by ants, coat the cupboard used for storing cakes with ant poison.

4. Storing icing tubes
Icing tubes are very expensive and should be properly cared for. The best method is to cover the bottom of the container in which you want to store them with a thin layer of Prestik (Plasticine adhesive) and stand the tubes upright. The lid of the container should not touch the tubes. Insert tubes in water immediately after use to prevent the icing sugar hardening inside. Carefully wash them later, preferably under running water, using a watercolour paintbrush. Do not allow children to lick the tubes or play with them as the tips damage and bend easily.

CHAPTER 4

Making the most of balance and colour

The impression a cake makes is determined mainly by the discriminating use of colour and whether a balance has been maintained. For this reason we would like to give some attention to these concepts.

A beginner is advised to draw a design on paper first and to decide which colour to use where. Otherwise all her hard work might be to no avail and she will not achieve the desired result. Her cake might look unbalanced.

Firstly, the cake board should be proportionately the right size for the cake – its diameter is usually 75 mm more than that of the cake. A larger board can, however, easily be balanced by repeating the decoration of the cake on the board, even if only in part. Extension work or filigree on the side of the cake also requires a bigger board. The height of the cake should be correct in relation to its diameter. If the cake appears a bit flat in relation to its diameter, a decoration such as a vase of flowers or a collar on pillars can give the cake extra height. Let us look at colour and balance in more detail.

1. Balance

When one thinks of balance, one automatically thinks of objects with the same mass (see Fig. 16).

Balance is, however, not only determined by the mass or size of an object. This is especially true when balance is determined visually – optical illusions should also be taken into account. For example, an object that is further away seems smaller than one that is nearer; straight lines that are supposedly parallel (such as railway lines) seem closer together the further away they are, etc. We know how visually irritating a painting which hangs askew, or an ornament too close to the wall or too many small objects arranged together on one side of a mantelpiece can be. Even the indiscriminate arrangement of furniture in a room can be disturbing. Although one is not always able to analyse precisely what is wrong, one instinctively feels uncomfortable. An object of beauty that is badly placed can be irritating.

The same can be said of a cake. The most attractive work can be a failure if the whole is not balanced. It might be that the flowers themselves or the floral arrangements on the cake are too heavy in relation to the cake or that the flowers may tilt too much to one side. This is such an important aspect that it cannot be over-stressed. Even if one creates the most beautiful flowers and has no understanding of balance, all the hard work may have been in vain.

Keep in mind, too, the difference between formal and informal balance, the symmetrical and asymmetrical arrangement of objects – the principles of balance must be maintained in both instances. The same principles apply to the arrangement of fresh flowers. In a formal arrangement the height and size of the flowers are in balance. The balance of an informal arrangement is achieved more subtly by arranging small and fewer flowers upright, and larger and darker flowers below, etc. The same kinds of flowers need not be used either. Compare the two floral arrangements in Fig. 17.

Although this type of arrangement would never be used for cakes, a grasp of the basic principles of balance is essential. Let us apply the same principles to cake decoration and analyse the illustrations in Fig. 18. (Note how balance is achieved by adding a few lines and curls.) Also study the cakes in Photographs 17-19 on pp. 97, 98 and 99.

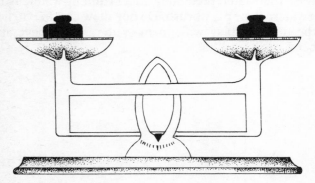
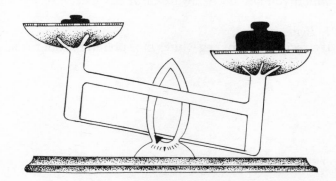

Fig. 16

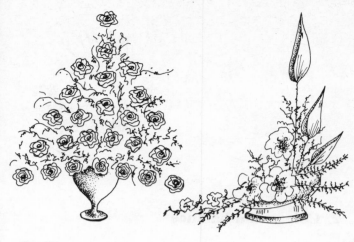

Fig. 17

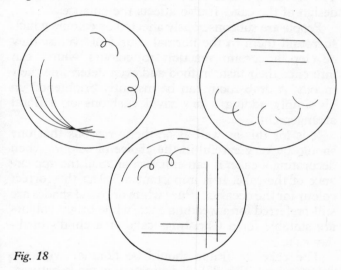

Fig. 18

just a suggestion of a soft floral filler is often more striking than a full-scale arrangement. This is especially true when one decorates with tube flowers – in which case too many flowers are to be avoided.

We would like to repeat that it is advisable for beginners first to draw a few possible designs on a piece of paper and then decide how to use the flowers. Let us look at an example: In Fig. 19a one large flower or three small roses with their leaves are shown in the centre of the cake. As there are not enough flowers for an entire arrangement they should be placed in the centre and to obtain the correct balance the rest of the cake should be decorated with Cornelli work or dots. In other words, this cake would be formal and symmetrical. Fig. 19b is an example of an informal or asymmetrical design where the writing balances the floral arrangement. In Fig. 19c the writing, which should be large and bold, balances the arrangement, while in Fig. 19d a very formal effect has been achieved.

Let us look at another example. First draw a few

Fig. 19

How does the arrangement of flowers on a cake affect the balance? As we have said, the same rules for fresh floral arrangements apply to the arrangement of flowers on a cake. However, there are other factors the cake decorator should keep in mind. While the arranger of fresh flowers only has to ensure that the size of the flowers fits the container, the cake decorator also has to ensure that the flowers are in the correct proportion to one another. She will, for example, not make arum lilies smaller than roses, or sweet peas larger than a hibiscus.

Another important principle is deciding on an informal or formal arrangement on the cake, and then keeping to the decision. Do not suddenly decide that, just because a beautiful large rose is available, it must be used somewhere at all costs, and spoil the entire balance of your arrangement. Decide what "lines" you want to use and keep to them. In cake decoration you have the advantage of being able to determine your lines with the tube and make flowers according to any required size.

Remember that a beautiful large single flower with

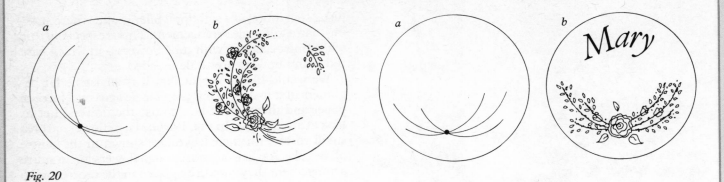

Fig. 20

curves to establish the "lines" (Fig. 20). Notice how all the lines cross at one point (Fig. 20a). This is the focal point where the large flower or bow should be positioned, with the smaller flowers and ferns placed further away. Opposite this point a small flower with a leaf or fern or even writing could then be positioned – with a few curls added for the correct balance (Fig. 20b).

In Fig. 21 we have a symmetrical pattern or formal arrangement. Divide the circle, which is the circumference of the cake, into eight equal sections and mark the design on the cake with pinpricks. Join the dots with curves that alternately curl in and out (Fig. 21a). Add symmetrical branches on the inside and outside (Fig. 21b) to ensure that the symmetrical balance of the design is maintained. Decide where the flowers should be positioned. The larger flowers (of the same kind) are placed on the dots with one pointing inwards and the following one outwards (Fig. 21c). Always keep the symmetry of the design in mind and place the leaves, and buds, if necessary, on the shorter branches (Fig. 21d). With this type of formal arrangement the writing can be placed in the centre.

When placing a vase with a floral arrangement on top of the cake for a change, ensure that the vase complements the other decorations. For example, a vase which is too heavy not only upsets the balance but also detracts attention from the flowers and other decorations.

2. Colour and balance

The correct use of colour is extremely important in the design of the cake. It also affects the balance.

People are subconsciously affected by colours which surround them in the normal course of events; they develop a certain reaction to colours which can influence their taste in food and even determine their moods. A drab room can be instantly brightened up by simply adding a few vivid cushions or a floral arrangement.

It is for this as well as aesthetic reasons that one should be very careful in the choice of colours when decorating a cake; it can enhance or spoil the appearance of the cake. It is important to select the correct colour for the occasion. Pure white or pastel shades are still preferred for a wedding cake, while bright colours are suitable for a Christmas cake or a child's birthday cake.

The cake decorator should be familiar with the colour wheel (Fig. 22). A distinction is made between the primary colours – red, yellow and blue – and the secondary colours – orange, green and purple. The secondary colours are obtained by mixing equal quantities of two primary colours. Red and yellow produce orange, blue and yellow produce green, and blue and red produce purple. Shades of secondary colours are obtained by adjusting the quantity and intensity of one of

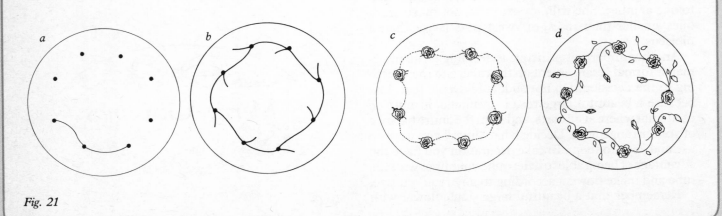

Fig. 21

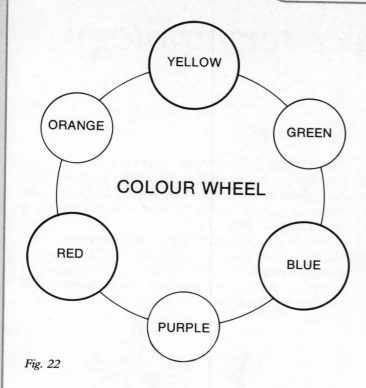

COLOUR WHEEL

YELLOW

ORANGE

GREEN

RED

BLUE

PURPLE

Fig. 22

example, more intense than yellow. Thus, when red is mixed with yellow, orange or green, less red than the other colour would be used in order to obtain a certain colour.

There are also complementary colours. These colours, like blue and orange or purple and yellow, are opposite each other on the colour wheel and produce grey when mixed. The shade of grey will be determined by the amount and intensity of the stronger of the colours used in the mixing process.

It is advisable that the beginner should keep to pastel shades when mixing colours. In this way one cannot easily go wrong. In the meantime, make a thorough study of colour.

Colour also influences balance; a dark or bright colour is "heavier" than a light colour. A dark colour should therefore be your focal point. A large flower as focal point can be balanced by a touch of dark colour amongst the smaller flowers or in the writing on the cake.

3. Balance in wedding cakes

When stacking cakes on top of each other, for example wedding cakes, the balance should receive special attention. The end result should form a pyramid once the individual cakes have been stacked and the proportions between the bottom, centre and top cakes should correspond with their respective sizes.

the primary colours. If, for example, more red than blue is added, the secondary colour will be a reddish purple; the other way round will give purple of a bluish shade.

When mixing colours, it should be kept in mind that the intensity of colours differs. Red and blue are, for

CHAPTER 5

Know the correct terminology

To ensure that the beginner will understand the terminology used later in this book, we would like to explain some terms used in cake decorating. It is also advisable for the beginner to become adept at these different techniques before attempting to decorate a cake.

1. Dots

This gives a very dainty finish to a cake. Proceed as follows: Keep a writing tube (especially No 1, 0 or 00) or a small star tube (No 5 or 6) upright close to the surface of the cake and pipe out a very small quantity of icing. *Stop piping* and quickly raise the tube.

The most common mistake made is that the dot is not flat but pointed. If this is the case, the point should be flattened immediately. Dots should really be dots only; there should be no points or tail ends. When a star tube is used, the dot is called a "star" (Fig. 23).

Fig. 23

2. Pillars

A pillar is made of dots which are stacked on top of one another, ranging from large to small (Fig. 24). The beginner is advised to pipe a whole row of dots first and to let them dry. Do the same with the following rows.

Once you are adept at the art you will be able to do it all in one flowing motion. The icing should be quite stiff, and therefore only royal icing is used for this purpose.

Fig. 24

3. Teardrops

The teardrop differs from the dot in that the tube is not kept upright but at a 45° angle when piping the icing. *Stop piping* as soon as you have piped a dot and pull the tube away against the cake to form a tail end which will later break off (Fig. 25).

Teardrops are usually piped with a writing tube, although a star tube (as indicated in Fig. 51 on p. 41) is sometimes used. Place two teardrops next to each other to form a heart. Three teardrops placed together will produce a *fleur-de-lys*.

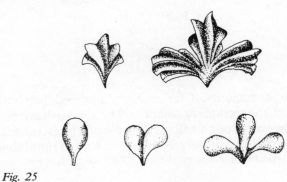

Fig. 25

4. Press and pull movement

Hold the tube against the cake at an angle, pipe out a very small quantity of icing, stop piping and pull the tube away against the cake so that the drop breaks off to form a tail end. Proceed by piping the next drop close enough to the preceding one for the drop of icing just to cover the tail end of the preceding drop. With practice this becomes a single flowing motion of press-stop-pull-move.

If this movement is carried out rhythmically and accurately so that all the drops are uniform, it can be used to pipe an attractive border around the bottom of a

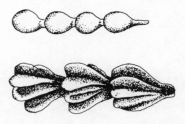

Fig. 26

cake or to finish some other decoration. If a writing tube is used, it is called a "snailstrail", while it is called a "shell" if a star or shell tube is used (Fig. 26).

In the chapter describing cake borders combinations of different movements are described.

5. The E-movement

Keeping the tube against the cake, pipe an even row of e's. Pull the tube right through the first part of the e when making the second part. The second part of the e should not go *over* the first part but *through* it. This is usually done with a writing or star tube (Fig. 27).

Fig. 27

6. Roping

A small star tube (No 5 or 6) is normally used, although a bigger writing tube (No 2 or 3) is also suitable.

A rope is in actual fact an elongated S lying on its side. The beginning of each S should be piped against the curve of the previous S – it should appear to start underneath the previous S. Every subsequent S should cover the end of the previous S (Fig. 28).

Fig. 28

7. Cornelli work

Use a small writing tube for this series of twists (No 1, 0 or 00). The work should be very fine and even but should not form a definite pattern. Long straight lines, dots or loops should be avoided. The lines should not cross one another (Fig. 29).

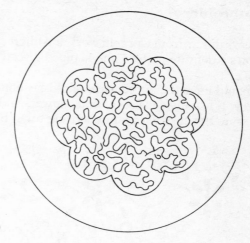

Fig. 29

This technique requires practice to perfect. It is a pretty, dainty finish and is also an easy way of disguising an uneven covering.

8. Filigree

Although filigree is quite advanced, we have included it for the beginner who wants to learn how to do a simple bit of filigree or even to make a few lace points (Fig. 30).

Fig. 30

Delicate filigree decorations are piped with a very fine tube on to a pattern covered with plastic sheeting. Once dry, the filigree decorations are loosened and transferred to the cake. With the necessary patience and practice any decorator can master this delicate form of sugarcraft. Ideally filigree should be gossamer fine, delicate, neat and even. There should be no joins and the points should be even and similar in appearance. Because such a fine tube is used for filigree, we recommend that you use the special royal icing on p. 17.

9. Embroidery

This work differs from Cornelli work and filigree in that it follows a definite pattern and is piped directly on to the cake.

It should have the appearance of old-fashioned embroidery. It usually consists of dots, flowers and leaves piped on to the cake with a fine writing tube (Fig. 31).

Fig. 31

10. Floodwork

There are different versions of floodwork but in all variations soft icing is allowed to flow into a pattern which has been piped in advance by means of a writing tube. Unusual effects can be obtained by using icing of different consistencies. Floodwork is used for loose figurines which can later be transferred to the cake and arranged in either a flat, raised or upright position. For a floodwork collar the outlines of a frame are piped with a writing tube and later filled with runny icing. It can either be placed directly on the cake or balanced on pillars on top of the cake.

Floodwork can be used for three-dimensional scenes but this is advanced work. The patterns at the back of this book include floodwork collars and a few figurines (Fig. 81-87 on pp. 129-136).

11. Basket weave

Basket weave looks complicated but it is actually quite simple (Fig. 32). A small star tube or a large writing tube is normally used. When done on the side of a cake, the correct basket weave tube (Tala No 34) must be used. Vertical lines can be done with a writing tube and horizontal lines with Tala tube No 34.

First pipe a vertical line (AB) and then pipe short horizontal lines (CD) across AB. Ensure that you pipe them one width apart so that the next line (GH) will fit neatly in between them. Pipe another vertical line (EF) so that it just covers the ends of the horizontal (CD). Pipe the horizontal lines (GH) between the previous horizontal lines (CD) to look as if they start *underneath line AB*. Continue until the cake is covered in basket weave.

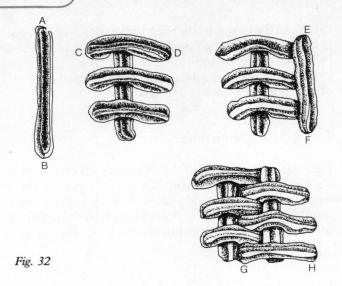

Fig. 32

12. Frills

A frill is usually piped against the side or on top of a cake (see Photograph 19 on p. 99). It can be piped directly against or on top of a cake by means of a petal tube (Tala No 11 or 18).

With the sharp end of the tube against the cake at a 45° angle, pipe out the icing while moving the tube evenly backwards and forwards. Always keep the sharp end on the line of the pattern which has been pricked beforehand. The upper line of the frill (the section which will be joined to the cake) is finished in snailstrail, dots or tiny shells (Fig. 33).

The Garrett frill is made from fondant paste and is slightly more advanced. It is described in detail on p. 42.

Fig. 33

13. Extension work

This decoration, piped with a very fine tube, is usually done around the bottom of a cake. First build a platform, usually crescent-shaped, around the bottom of the cake, and then make the lines (bridge lines) from a central point or a point higher up against the side of the cake to the platform. Finish the bridge lines with small lace points or loops (Fig. 34). Extension work is discussed in detail on p. 62.

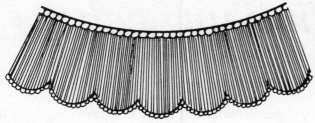

Fig. 34

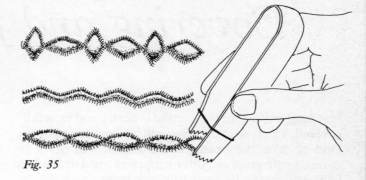

Fig. 35

14. Crimping

This decoration is made by means of crimpers (see p. 25). The crimper is pressed into the soft fondant and the ends are pinched together to crimp the fondant into a specific pattern (Fig. 35). The technique and finishing of crimping are most important and are discussed in full on p. 61.

15. Cocoa painting

This technique involves painting a mixture of cocoa and cocoa butter directly on to the cake or plaque with a fine paintbrush. It is described in detail on p. 42.

Although there are many other terms and techniques, these are the basic ones most used by beginners.

CHAPTER 6

Covering and finishing cakes

It is most important that a cake is neatly and tastefully covered. The type of covering will be determined by the kind of cake. For example, a fruitcake will never be covered with glacé or butter icing, and royal or fondant icing will never be used to cover layer cakes. In the following section we will discuss how to cover cakes with different types of icing. (The recipes for the different types of icing appear in Chapter 2.)

1. Covering cakes

CRUMBS, COCONUT AND NUTS AS SIDE COVERING
Biscuit crumbs, roasted coconut or chopped nuts make a most attractive and delicious finish for butter and sponge cakes.

Crumbs: Using a rolling-pin, roll the biscuits into relatively fine crumbs – not as fine as flour but not too coarse either.

Roasted coconut: In a frying pan, add 12,5 ml cooking oil and 10 ml sugar to 200 g fine coconut. Mix well and stir while slowly roasting the coconut over moderate heat. It should not be too brown.

Chopped nuts: Finely chop the nuts and roll on a hard surface with a rolling-pin. Chopped nuts slightly roasted in a moderate oven (remember to stir them every now and then) add a delicious flavour to a cake.

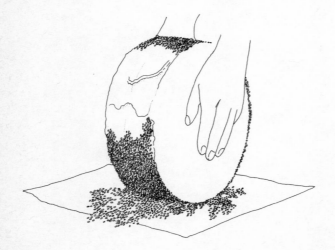

Fig. 36

Cover the sides of the cake as follows (Fig. 36): First coat the sides of the cake with a thin layer of melted apricot jam or diluted icing. Pile the crumbs, coconut or nuts on a piece of waxed paper. Holding the cake between the hands, firmly roll it in the covering until the sides are well covered. Use a spatula to press the covering to the sides of the cake. Ensure that none of the covering sticks to the top of the cake. If this happens, carefully remove it with a dry tea towel or soft brush.

GLACÉ ICING COVERING

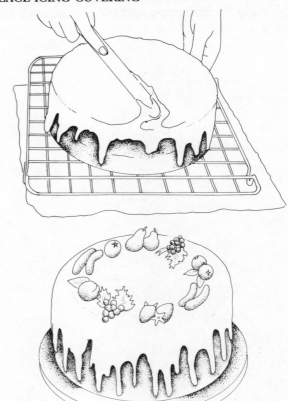

Fig. 37

Because this icing is very runny and quickly forms a crust, it should be poured over the cake as soon as it has been made. If necessary it could be spread over the cake with a knife dipped in hot water. Collect any remaining icing by placing the cake on a wire rack over a bowl or tray. A very attractive finish is achieved by letting the icing run down the sides of the cake in "tears". No further decoration is needed with this icing. A few pieces of glacé fruit add an attractive finish (Fig. 37).

FEATHERING AND MARBLING

Glacé icing looks most attractive when applied in the following manner. Melt a few pieces of cooking chocolate and add it to some of the glacé icing, or mix the icing with a little strong black coffee. Fill an icing bag with the mixture. Pour the white glacé icing over the cake and cut off the point of the icing bag containing the chocolate icing before it sets. Draw parallel lines or concentric circles on the cake with the chocolate icing. The chocolate icing should be warm enough to melt into the white icing and you should work quickly before the white icing sets.

In the cake with parallel lines, a fan effect can be achieved by drawing lines first in one direction and then in the opposite direction with a toothpick or knitting needle. Divide the second cake into eight equal sections and quickly mark them on the outside edge. Pipe concentric circles in chocolate. Draw eight lines across the chocolate circles from the centre of the cake to the outer edge and then, in the opposite direction, draw eight lines between these lines from the outer edge of the cake to its centre (Fig. 38). This is called marbling or feathering.

BUTTER ICING

This icing is used only for butter and sponge cakes (see the recipe on p. 16), never for fruitcakes. The sides of a layer cake are never covered with any icing other than a thin coating for coconut, crumbs or chopped nuts (see p. 34). The filling for a layer cake should be so delicious and attractive that it should appear to be part of the decoration. If you want to decorate the cake further, smooth the surface with a knife dipped in hot water and leave for a while.

ALMOND PASTE AND MARZIPAN

There are various ways to coat a fruitcake with marzipan. Whichever method you follow it is important that this covering should be applied thoroughly and evenly as it serves as the foundation for further decoration. If the undercoat is not applied properly the end product will suffer.

Before applying the undercoat you should consider the shape of the cake. A cake with a hump in the centre should be cut straight and turned upside down before being covered. Fill uneven parts or hollows in the cake with marzipan.

Spread over the cake a very thin layer of melted apricot jam or a beaten egg white to which 12,5 ml icing sugar has been added. Use an ordinary wide brush to apply the jam or egg white.

A marzipan undercoat for royal or plastic icing can be applied in two ways:

Method 1: Spread the sides of the cake with jam or egg white. Take approximately one third of the marzipan and roll out an oblong strip on a surface that has been dusted with icing sugar. The marzipan should be between 6 mm and 12 mm thick. Cut a strip the height of the cake and the length of the cake's circumference. Cut the two ends straight. Pick up the cake and roll it along the strip, letting it cling to the cake (Fig. 39).

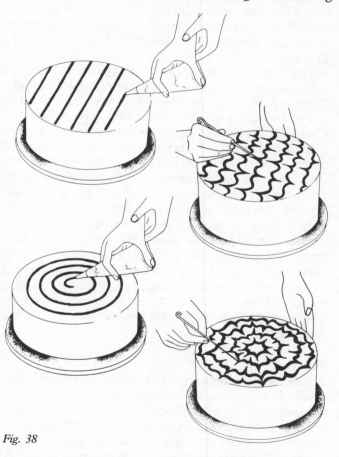

Fig. 38

It is also a most effective decoration for cupcakes or muffins. Instead of chocolate, different colours of piping gel can be used (see Photograph 17 on p. 97).

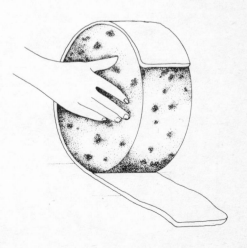

Fig. 39

Roll out the remaining marzipan into a large, round, flat shape as thick as the side strip. Measure the diameter of the cake, including the marzipan covering the sides. Cut out a round pattern according to this measurement, place it on the rolled-out marzipan and cut out a circle. Lift it carefully and position it on top of the cake. Rub down well. Carefully cut off any sections overlapping the edge of the cake once the circle has been rubbed down. Rub the edge of the cake until it is rounded if the cake is to be covered with plastic icing. If royal icing is to be used, ensure that the edge is sharp. Rub the marzipan with the palm of your hand until it is smooth and shiny and leave for at least 24 hours before covering it with more icing.

Method 2: Roll out a piece of marzipan on a surface dusted with icing sugar. It should be larger than the diameter of the cake. Coat the top of the cake (in actual fact the bottom of the cake, which in the case of fruitcakes is always more even than the top and thus more suitable for decorating) with jam or egg white. Turn the cake upside down and put the coated surface on the rolled-out marzipan. Carefully cut out the marzipan against the edge of the cake. Remove any excess marzipan. Carefully turn the cake over. Coat the sides with jam or egg white. Roll out a strip the height of the cake and the length of the cake's circumference. Cut the sides and ends of the strip straight. Roll up the strip and then unroll it against the side of the cake (Fig. 40). Rub down as explained in the first method.

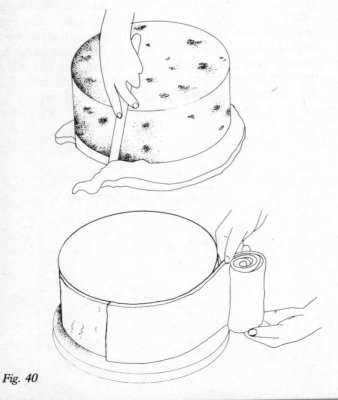

Fig. 40

Method 3: Marzipan can also be used as covering on its own and is delicious with a spiced cake.

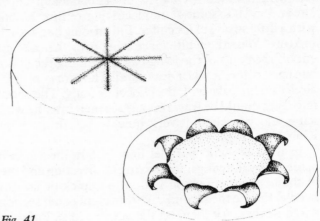

Fig. 41

Spread the cake with melted apricot jam, ensuring that there is a thick layer of jam in the centre of the cake. Put a piece of waxed paper 75 mm in diameter on top of the jam in the centre of the cake. Roll out the marzipan into a flat piece approximately 10 mm thick and large enough to cover the entire cake. Measure the diameter of the cake board and add twice the height of the cake plus another 20 mm; this is the diameter of the circle to be cut. First cut out a paper pattern, place it on top of the rolled-out marzipan and cut out the circle accordingly. Place a rolling-pin on one end of the circle and roll approximately a quarter of it around the rolling-pin. Carefully lift the rolling-pin with the marzipan and place it on the cake. (The marzipan can also be picked up by inserting two stiff pieces of cardboard to lift the marzipan and place it on top of the cake. Remove the two pieces of cardboard gently.) Carefully fix the marzipan to the cake by pressing it down lightly and rubbing it down the sides of the cake until it touches the cake board. Make a few cuts in the middle of the marzipan on top of the cake (Fig. 41). Curl the ends of the "star" to the outside and carefully remove the piece of waxed paper on top of the jam. Finish the cake by piping a shell border in royal icing on the board around the bottom of the cake (see p. 40). Pipe dots on the edges of the star.

FONDANT OR PLASTIC ICING
Knead the icing thoroughly. It should be so pliable that it will show no cracks when made into a roll and folded or stretched. Wipe the almond layer with a damp cloth until it feels sticky, or coat it with a little egg white mixed with 5 ml icing sugar. Knead the icing again, but do not fold it over as for pastry; too much air is trapped this way. On a surface dusted with icing sugar, roll out the icing in one large piece, approximately 12 mm thick. Determine the diameter of the required circle as fol-

lows: Measure from one edge of the cake board over the top of the cake to the opposite edge of the board. Draw a circle with this circumference on a piece of paper. Place the pattern on the icing and cut it out. Roll a section of it over a rolling-pin, carefully pick it up and place it on top of the cake. Rub down the icing, using the palm of your hand or a piece of muslin. Rub down the sides as well and cut off the excess icing around the bottom of the cake.

Note: Unless the circle has been cut too small, there will always be fondant left over as it stretches when smoothed over the cake. Check the icing for any air-bubbles and prick them by inserting a needle at an angle. Gently rub out any air. Using the palm of your hand or a piece of muslin, rub the icing until it is smooth. A piece of equipment designed especially to smooth icing is available commercially.

2. The borders of the cake

TOP BORDER
If the cake is covered with plastic icing a border is usually not necessary around the top edge of the cake, although a delicate crimped or filigree border is some-times used. (See p. 38 and Chapter 10 for a detailed dis-cussion of these two techniques.) Dots or Cornelli work are sometimes piped on the top edge of the cake.

Where butter or glacé icing has been used to cover only the top surface of a cake, an attractive border adds the finishing touch.

Figure 8 or S scrolls
This pattern is piped with a star tube (No 5, 6 or 8). The decoration on top of the cake will determine how heavy the border can be without upsetting the balance. A large or small tube will be used accordingly. Pipe out the icing evenly and slowly move the tube in the shape of a figure 8 lying on its side. Stop piping when nearly at the end of the figure 8, breaking off the icing without forming a point. If there is a little point, flatten it with your finger. (This will, however, be an indication that you kept on piping for too long.) Line the scrolls up against each other, taking care not to stretch the scroll itself. This pattern can be complemented by a line or dots along the bottom or the top (Fig. 42) of the scrolls.

Fig. 42

Reverse scroll
A reverse scroll is in fact half a scroll that first turns inwards and then outwards. Using a star tube, pipe out a star. As soon as the icing adheres to the cake, move the tube in a semicircle to the outside and stop piping more or less immediately, finishing the scroll with a tail end against the edge of the cake. Repeat the same movement but move to the inside, ensuring that the star overlaps the tail end of the previous scroll (Fig. 43).

Fig. 43

The E-movement
This pattern (Fig. 44) is discussed in detail on p. 31. When done with a No 13 tube, the decoration resembles miniature roses.

Fig. 44

Roping
This decoration is discussed on p. 31.

Scroll combinations
Many interesting effects can be obtained by combining scrolls, teardrops, dots and lines (Fig. 45 and Photo-graph 4 on p. 38). There are a few patterns for different combinations at the back of the book, but try experi-menting with your own ideas.

Fig. 45

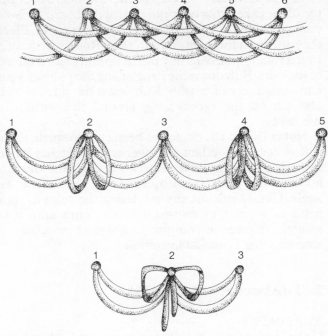

Photograph 4

Fig. 46

Draped lines or loops

These designs can soften the appearance of a cake (see Photograph 5) especially when piped with a fine tube (No 1, 0 or 00) in different colours.

Note: Bold lines were used in Fig. 46 to make it easier to follow. A fine tube should, however, be used.

Pipe a series of small dots close to the top edge of the cake, ensuring that they are evenly spaced and in a straight line. Secure the icing to the third dot. Return to the second dot, secure the icing to it and pipe another loop, securing it to the fourth dot. Pipe loops right round the cake, ensuring that they are uniform.

You can have more loops crossing each other: Starting at the first dot, secure the loop to the fourth dot. Pipe the following loop between the second and fifth dots, the third loop between the third and sixth dots, etc. If you have three icing bags with tubes of the same size but filled with different colours of icing, you can use them alternately to obtain a stunning rainbow effect.

Study the examples in Fig. 46 and try your own variations. The bows are secured to a single dot, but in the case of the "open" bow it can also be secured to the cake.

Crimping

Crimping is briefly mentioned in Chapter 5 and is discussed in detail in Chapter 10.

Filigree

Although filigree is discussed in Chapter 5, it deserves mentioning here as the beginner can make use of this advanced technique.

In addition to lace points that can be used with crimping or embroidery work, you can attach simple filigree pieces to the side of the cake. Proceed as follows (Photograph 6a, b and c). Place the pattern (see back of book) on top of a carton cake board or any other rigid surface. Secure a piece of plastic sheeting (the kind used for covering books) over the pattern with a few dots of royal icing or with drawing pins. *Using the icing for fine tubes* (see p. 17) and tube Nos 1, 0 and 00, accurately pipe the pattern on to the plastic sheeting and allow it to dry (a). Carefully loosen the plastic sheeting from the board, lift

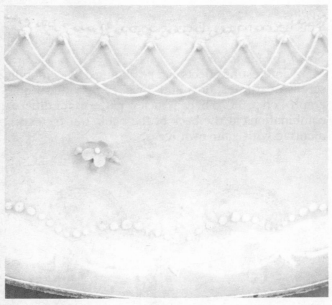

Photograph 5

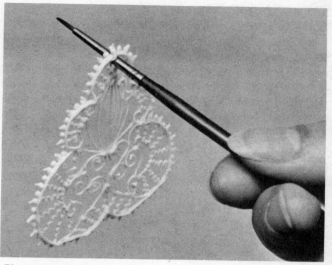

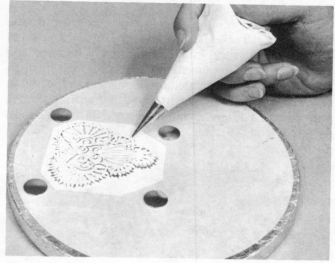

Photograph 6a

Photograph 6c

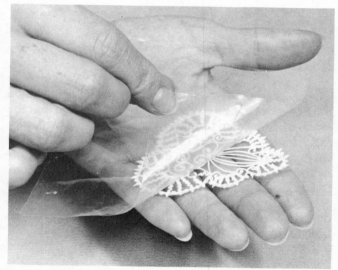

Photograph 6b

work is a border in itself). The bottom border can also be used to balance the entire cake. If, for example, the cake is a little too high in relation to its diameter, the bottom border can be extended on to the cake board to create the necessary balance.

Star tube scrolls
Star scrolls on a bottom border are piped in exactly the same way as those on a top border (see variations on p. 37). Ensure that the top and bottom borders complement each other even if the bottom border is heavier than the top. Fig. 47 illustrates one possible combination of scrolls, lines and dots. Try experimenting with your own designs.

it and carefully turn it on to the palm of your hand. Remove the plastic (b). Pipe dots at the places where you want to position the filigree and secure them to the cake. Remember to pick up the filigree at the point where it is most sturdy, or use a small brush to pick it up (c). If necessary, support the filigree with pieces of foam rubber.

BOTTOM BORDER
The bottom border, which secures the cake to the cake board, is most important as it adds a finish to the icing. Once again the type of decoration on top and against the sides of the cake will determine whether the bottom border should be lightly or heavily decorated. Usually the decoration is quite heavy (except in extension work where a delicate finish is required since the extension

Fig. 47

Extension border
This is one of the most attractive borders but requires a great deal of practice. It is discussed in detail on p. 62.

Shells and shell variations

Shells are the most frequently used decoration on bottom borders. It is worthwhile to master this press-pull movement for which the star or shell tube (Fig. 48) is used. There are very few decorators who do it correctly – note that you should not lift up the tube nor move it to and fro. Pipe out a drop of icing while keeping the tube against the cake at an angle of approximately 45°. *Stop piping* once the icing forms a nice round drop, pull the tube away, keeping it against the cake, and break the icing off to form a little tail end. Move the tube a few millimetres from the drop and repeat the procedure, ensuring that this drop only just covers the tail end of the previous shell (a).

Finish the shell border by piping a dot in between each shell or by piping semicircles at the top or bottom of the shells (b). You can also pipe a teardrop against the cake by using a star or shell tube and finish it with lines or dots (c). A round "fan" piped between the shells with leaf tube No 11 is also most effective (d).

Zigzag border

This is an easy yet effective way to pipe a border around the bottom of a cake. Using a star tube, pipe with a slight up and down zigzag movement. Slowly increase and then decrease the movement. The icing will form an oval-shaped pattern which distinctly shows the zigzag movement. Outline the pattern with a writing tube in the same or a different colour. A few dots are also most effective (Fig. 49).

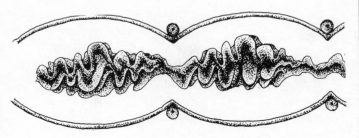

Fig. 49

3. The sides of the cake

The decoration for the sides of a cake will be determined by the type of icing you use. We have mentioned that the sides of a layer cake should never be decorated with piping. Piping on the sides of a cake is therefore limited to cakes covered with plastic or royal icing. As with Cornelli work or dots covering the entire surface of the cake, the decoration can be allowed to hang over the top edge of the cake to give the impression of a cloth that has been draped over the cake. In that case the cloth can be finished with a frill or a lace point.

Line work

The same line pattern described on p. 38 can be piped against the sides of the cake.

Chandelier

This decoration reminds one of the beautiful glass crystals hanging from large chandeliers. It consists of teardrops which are piped with a small star tube from the bottom to the top on the side of the cake. Ensure that they are well spaced and uniform – they should not be too large for then they will be too heavy. Join the ends of

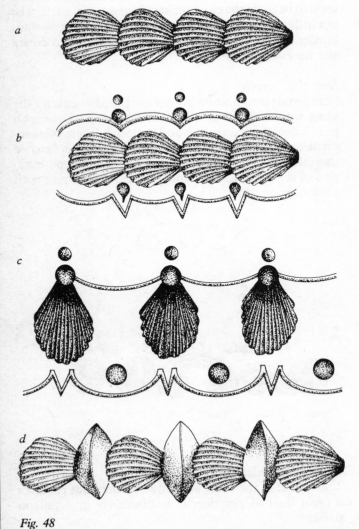

Fig. 48

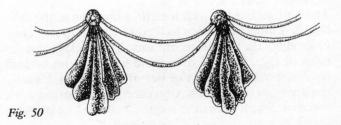

Fig. 50

the chandeliers with loops and pipe a dot on each end (Fig. 50). The same decoration can be piped upside down against the sides of a cake.

Fleur-de-lys

To pipe a *fleur-de-lys*, slightly curved teardrops are joined together (Fig. 51). This can be done with a star or writing tube, but the piping should be very delicate – definitely not bold! Finish it by finely outlining the pattern.

We have supplied a few variations – but never use two different variations on one cake. Always take care not to over-decorate the sides of a cake.

 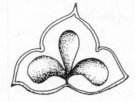

Fig. 51

Embroidery work

Simple embroidery work can be used to good effect on the sides of a cake provided it is not overdone and complements the rest of the decoration. We recommend that the beginner keeps to simple flowers, possibly combining them with semicircles or crimping (Fig. 52). But remember: rather too little than too much!

Fig. 52

Photograph 7a

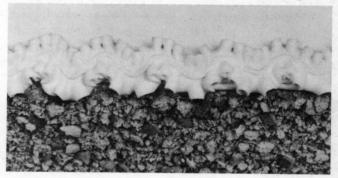

Photograph 7b

Frills

A frill is a popular finish for Cornelli or embroidery work. On its own against the sides of a cake too it looks stunning. (See Photograph 7a and b.)

There are different kinds of frills:

- A frill that is piped directly on to the cake.

Use Tala tubes No 10, 11 or 18 (or corresponding tubes in different makes) and proceed as follows: Measure the circumference of the cake with a long strip of paper approximately 80 mm wide. Fold the paper into six or eight sections. Fold it in half once again and cut out a semicircle of the required size and depth. Keeping it against the side of the cake, prick the scallops right around the cake. Ensure that the pattern is always the same distance from the cake board or else the pattern will be lopsided.

Fill the icing bag containing the tube. Holding the No 10 tube against the cake, pipe firmly and follow the pattern pricked on the cake. If using tubes No 11 or 18, the sharp end should be held with the tip touching the cake and the rest of the tube should be held at a 45° angle to the cake. Evenly move the tube to and fro, following the pricked pattern with the tip of the tube. The frills in Fig.

53a and Fig. 53b were piped with a No 10 tube and Nos 11 and 18 tubes respectively.

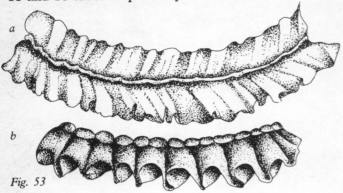

Fig. 53

• Garrett frill (by courtesy of Elaine Garrett).

Add a little gum tragacanth or CMC to a small piece of plastic icing and roll it out thinly. Using a biscuit cutter with a diameter of approximately 70 mm, cut a circle. Inside this circle cut out another circle with a 20 mm diameter. Cut through the circle and carefully open it out. Using a toothpick or knitting needle, flute the outer edge of the circle (Fig. 54). Carefully pick up the frill and, using a little royal icing, secure it to the pricked semicircles against the side of the cake (see Photograph 39 on p. 119). Finish the top section of the frill with small shells or snailstrail.

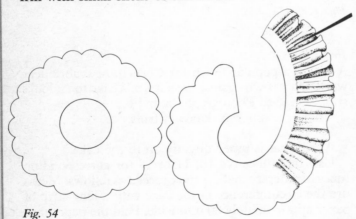

Fig. 54

Ribbon inserts (Fig. 55)
As this technique (Photograph 8) is mostly used with filigree or crimping, it is described in detail in Chapter 10.

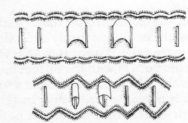

Fig. 55

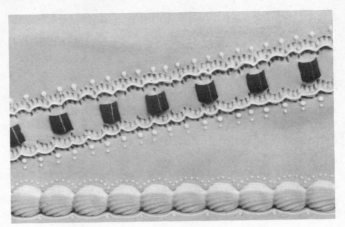

Photograph 8

4. Cocoa painting

Cocoa painting can be done on top or against the sides of a cake provided the surface is even and it is done on royal icing, plastic icing, floodwork or *pastillage*. It can be freehand or a design can be lightly traced on to the cake before starting. Using a very soft pencil, trace the design on to tracing paper, turn the paper over and repeat the lines. Turn the paper face down on the cake and gently rub the lines on to the cake. The actual painting is done with fine paintbrushes. Their thickness will depend on the design.

Melt 5 ml cocoa butter over hot water. Put approximately 5 ml cocoa next to the melted cocoa butter. Using a paintbrush, mix it to the required colour. Mix different shades of brown. An interesting effect can be achieved by painting certain parts with more than one coat, or by using a sharp knife to carve out finer detail. If cocoa butter is unobtainable, ordinary vegetable fat can be used instead.

The horse decoration on the side of the cake in Photograph 9 and Photograph 38 (p. 118) is a good example of this technique.

Photograph 9

CHAPTER 7

Flowers piped directly on to the cake

In Chapter 4 we discussed how to design a cake. We will devote this chapter to the making of different types of flower and will explain how to pipe them directly on to the cake. These flowers are only used on layer cakes, although the busy homemaker could also successfully use royal icing to pipe them on to a fruitcake covered with plastic icing.

In Chapter 8 we will explain how to make beautiful flowers in royal icing on flower nails. These as well as modelled flowers (Chapter 11) can be used on a fruitcake, while the flowers discussed in this chapter should only be used on soft cakes, even if it is possible to make them in royal icing.

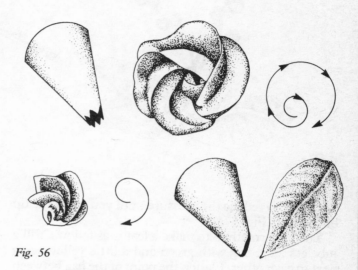

Fig. 56

1. Rose

The rose has always been the cake decorator's favourite flower. Although there are many methods of making it, this is by far the easiest and least time-consuming. Obviously it cannot be compared to a hand-modelled rose or even roses made on a flower nail, but it looks fine in butter icing.

Proceed as follows: Fill the bag containing a No 13 Tala tube with icing in two colours next to each other, for example white and rose pink or pale pink and pale yellow. The colours will mix to produce beautiful shades.

Keeping the bag vertical, pipe while making an even circular movement with the tube to form a rose. Do not close the centre (starting point) of the flower. Stop piping just before the circle is completed. Move the tube against the cake as you complete the circle until the icing breaks off.

Remember, practice makes perfect. Also remember that No 13 is the only tube really suitable for making a rose – the other star tubes either have too many or too few serrations.

A rosebud or miniature rose is made in the same way, except that a more abrupt movement is used, almost like making a comma. These miniature roses, with or without leaves, make an exquisite border.

To make a rose-leaf, use green icing and a No 11 Tala tube. To obtain the correct shade of green, put a little yellow or even brown icing in the bag next to the green icing.

The slanted tip of the tube should touch the cake,

almost as if you are trying to prevent the icing running out. Pipe very gently, allowing the icing to bulge out on both sides; stop piping and move the tube slightly. Repeat the procedure. The last pressure applied should be very slight. With a little practice you should be able to execute the entire procedure in a single movement. Take care not to give the leaf too much of an elongated shape – a rose-leaf is rounded. There are other ways of making leaves, but these we will discuss later. This leaf is, however, the closest to a real rose-leaf (see Fig. 56).

2. Hollyhock

This simple yet attractive flower is useful when you need flowers to decorate the walls or garden of, for example, a Hänsel and Gretel house.

Use green icing and a No 2 tube to pipe a stem. Use the No 2 tube for the flowers as well and make simple dots on and against the stem. Give the dots a slight twist but do not make a tail end. If you do not have an extra No 2 tube, fill a bag which has no tube with the icing and simply cut off the point.

Hollyhock leaves can be made in two different ways. Using a No 2 tube, pipe out a blob of icing. Slowly move the tube in the curve of the leaf and gradually reduce the pressure. This is one half of the leaf. Repeat the same movement on the other side. The join between the two halves form the centre vein of the leaf. Remember

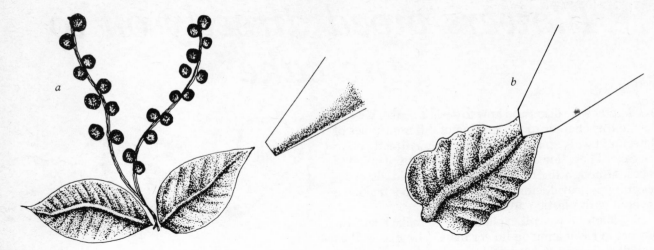

Fig. 57

gradually to reduce the pressure until you reach the tip of the leaf (Fig. 57a).

The other method to make a leaf is as follows. Fill a tubeless icing bag with green and a little yellow icing next to each other. Flatten the point of the bag between your fingers and cut it away on either side (Fig. 57b). Keeping the point of the bag flat, press out some icing. (The icing will bulge out at both sides.) Gradually reduce the pressure while moving the bag until the icing breaks off to form a tail end.

3. Salvia

This simple little flower, usually made in pale purple or yellow, is very effective as it enhances the lines of an arrangement and softens the effect. It simply consists of a row of dots arranged in a slight curve from large to small.

Remember to keep the dots flat, uniform and touching each other (see Fig. 58). Salvias are always used with other flowers to give the arrangement an attractive line.

4. Snowdrop

For this flower we use the popular No 2 tube. First pipe the stem in a slight curve in green icing. Also pipe the long, straight leaves with the No 2 tube. Reduce the pressure when you get to the top of the leaf and let it curl over and downwards when you stop piping and raise the tube from the cake. Flatten the leaves slightly with your finger.

Make the flowers at the end of the slightly curved stem as follows. Pipe two teardrops against each other in white icing (see p. 30) and let the ends curl up slightly before raising the tube. Pipe a third teardrop directly on top of the previous two teardrops. Allow the teardrops to dry and with a small paintbrush paint a tiny green dot on the end of each leaf (see Fig. 59a).

5. Lily of the valley

This small, delicate flower is made in the same way as the snowdrop except that the "drops" are now single teardrops piped against the stem, ranging from big to small (Fig. 59). It can also be made in the same way as the bluebell described below.

Fig. 58

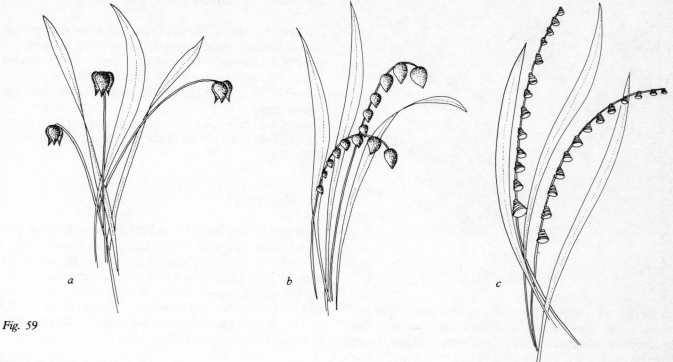

Fig. 59

6. Bluebell

This tiny flower is made in pale blue. Arrange the bells from large (at the bottom) to small (at the top). Use a No 1 tube and build up the bells by making a spiral movement against the stem, from the bottom to the top. The end result should resemble small bells hanging from the stem (Fig. 59).

7. Forget-me-not

This delicate flower can be made in no time with a special tube (Tala No 28). Keep the tube vertical against the

cake, pipe once, stop piping and lift the tube. If you do not have this tube, you can still make the flowers by simply piping a circle of five dots with a No 2 tube (Fig. 60). Ensure that there are no tail ends on the dots. Finish the flowers with a yellow dot in the centre. You need not use a tube for these yellow dots – simply fill the bag with yellow icing and cut off the point.

8. Queen Anne's lace

Queen Anne's lace softens an arrangement. First pipe the stem by using a No 2 tube filled with green icing. Then pipe a few delicate branches in the shape of an

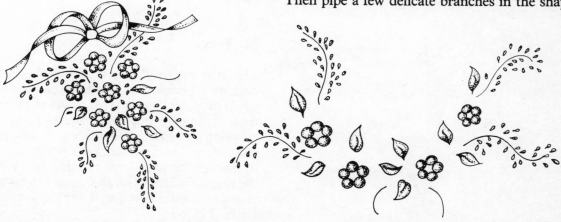

Fig. 60

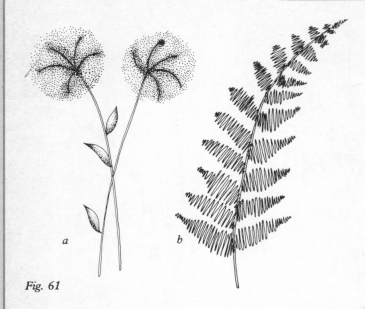

Fig. 61

10. Ears of wheat

Dark brown ears of wheat are beautiful amongst yellow or blue flowers. First pipe a dark brown stem by means of a No 2 tube and then make teardrops for the grains (see p. 30): first on the stem, then from the bottom all along the stem and later criss-cross to make the ear round and fat at the bottom and slender at the top. Using a No 1 tube, pipe lines running outwards from the grains. Take care not to make the ears look too heavy (Fig. 62a).

11. Bulrush

This reed is very simple to make but most effective. Use dark brown icing and a No 2 tube. First pipe a slightly curved stem. Pipe the head of the reed at the top of the stem by piping out a thick blob of icing and slowly moving the tube along the stem. Stop piping as soon as the head is formed and pull the tube away to form the tail end at the tip. The leaves are piped in the same way as those of the snowdrop (Fig. 62b).

umbrella with a No 1 tube. Using the same tube and white icing, pipe fine dots around the branches. Obviously the cake should be covered with a coloured icing for the dots to be visible (Fig. 61).

9. Ferns

Ferns are ideal for arrangements. Pipe the stem in green icing with a No 1 tube, then make a zigzag movement away from the stem, ending in dots (Fig. 61b).

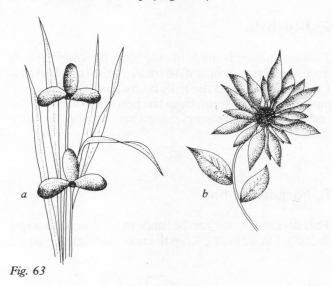

Fig. 63

12. Iris

This magnificent flower is among the easiest to pipe because a special tube (Tala No 4) can be used. Pipe the stems first and then pipe the leaves in the same way as those of the snowdrops. Keep the tube and the icing bag containing purple or yellow icing at right angles to the point of the stem and right against the cake – as if trying to prevent the icing from running out. Pipe, allowing the icing to bulge out on all three sides. Stop piping and remove the tube. A yellow dot in the centre adds a nice finish (Fig. 63a).

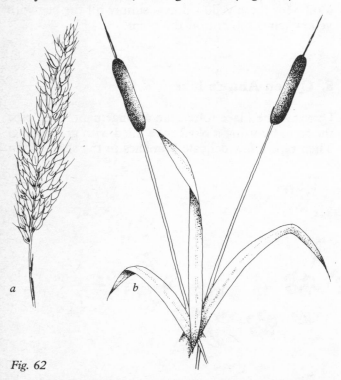

Fig. 62

13. Poinsettia

These bright red flowers look stunning, especially on a Christmas cake. To obtain a deep red colour, use only paste colouring or the icing will become too soft. It is unnecessary to pipe stems as you will only need to make one flower and a few leaves. Pipe the petals by means of a No 2 tube. First pipe a large dot of green icing for the centre of the flower. Pipe the petals in red icing by adjusting the pressure on the bag in the following way. Begin by applying slight pressure, increase the pressure, decrease the pressure and eventually stop the pressure. The petals vary from large to quite small and are first piped flat on to the cake, later overlapping each other. Note that the petals do not touch. Space them so that seven or eight petals fit around the crown. Remember not to make them all the same size. Finish the flower with a few yellow dots on the green crown. The poinsettia leaves are made in the same way with green icing (Fig. 63b).

14. Bunches of grapes

Use a No 26 tube, but if that is not available a No 2

standby will do. Decide on the shape of the bunch in advance and begin by first piping the grapes (upside down teardrops) at the bottom of the bunch. Position each grape so that it overlaps the tail end of the preceding grape. Leave the icing to dry for a while when you have piped one layer of grapes. Then pipe another few grapes on top of the bottom grapes to give the bunch an attractive, rounded shape. Pipe a few leaves with a bag of which the point has been cut off (see Fig. 57 and description on p. 44). Finish the bunch by piping a few curly vines, using a No 1 tube and green icing. The grapes can be purple, a pale yellow-green or even the colour of the cake if they are to decorate the sides (Fig. 64a).

15. Holly

It is difficult to imagine a Christmas cake without holly. Colour the icing with red paste colouring and pipe fairly large round dots with a No 2 or 3 tube. Pipe the leaves by using green icing and a paper bag with the point cut off (see Fig. 57 and description on p. 44). Use a toothpick to give the leaves their characteristic pointed shape (Fig. 64b).

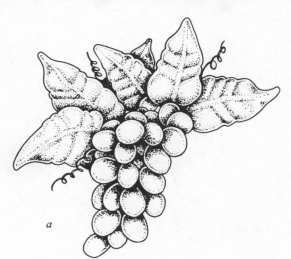

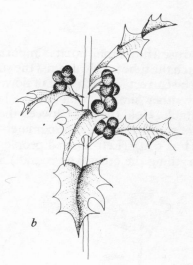

a

b

Fig. 64

CHAPTER 8

Piped flowers on flower nails

Beautiful flowers in royal icing can easily be piped on to flower nails and stored over a long period for use on cakes covered with plastic or royal icing.

1. Preparation

The texture of the royal icing is most important. It should not be too soft, otherwise the flowers will lose their shape, nor too stiff or the outer edges of the petals will crumble as they are piped from the tube. Colour the icing beforehand and keep it in an airtight container.

Cut out squares of waxed paper on which to make the flowers. Keep handy a few egg containers, bent pieces of tin and polystyrene containers used for packing apples on which to dry the flowers, as well as a cardboard box for storing them.

2. Technique

It is quite easy to use a flower nail but it is important that the angle at which the tube is held against the surface of the nail should be correct for each type of flower. A No 18 Tala or any other similar petal tube – larger or smaller – is suitable. Hold the nail between the thumb and forefinger of your left hand, approximately 30 mm from its head (Fig. 65a). (Left-handed people will obviously do everything the other way round.) Secure a

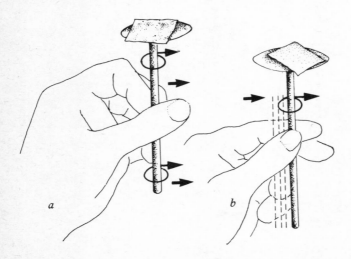

Fig. 65

square of waxed paper to the top of the nail with a dot of royal icing and flatten it. With the icing bag and tube in your right hand, pipe out the icing while slowly twirling the nail from left to right (see Fig. 65b). Carefully remove the paper from the flower nail and leave on a flat surface to dry. Remove the remaining paper from the flower once it is dry.

3. Peach and apple blossoms

These delicate florets consist of five small uniform pink (peach) and white (apple) petals.

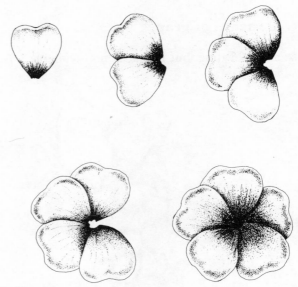

Fig. 66

Proceed as follows once you have secured the paper to the flower nail. Hold the bag containing the icing and the tube in your right hand. Keep the wide end of the tube against the nail and the sharp end at a 45° angle. Start in the centre of the square. Slowly twirl the flower nail while applying medium pressure and making a small circular movement with the tube. The wide end of the tube remains more or less stationary, although there should be a slight movement from the inside to the outside to make a curled petal. Pipe the remaining four petals in the same way. Remember that the petals should overlap slightly. Finish the blossom by piping a small yellow dot in the centre (Fig. 66).

4. Impatiens

These delightful little flowers come in many colours –
from deep pink, purple and yellow to snow white. They
differ from blossoms in that they have a slight point in
the centre of the two top petals. This point is made by
moving the tube slightly outward and then immediately
back to the centre of the petal. The two top petals
overlap slightly, while the two petals flanking them are
detached from the others and do not have any points.
The bottom petal is much broader than the others and
has a small indentation in the middle. A yellow-green
dot in the centre adds the finishing touch (Fig. 67).

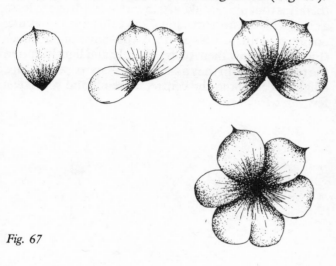

Fig. 67

5. Violets

These demure little flowers are piped in a deep purple
icing. The petals are not quite as rounded as those of the
blossoms. The three top petals overlap. The two bottom
petals are detached from the others and are slightly
more pointed. The curve made with the tube is not as
wide as for the top petals so the tube is moved up and
down rather than in a circular motion. The stamens are
made by piping two yellow dots in the centre (Fig.
68).

Fig. 68

Fig. 69

6. African violets

Although African violets and violets belong to the same
family, the two plants differ completely. The petals of
the African violet are much more fluted. This fluted
effect is achieved by quickly moving the icing tube up
and down while piping the curve. Any colour may be
used. Position the petals, which are all quite large, rounded and fluted, as follows. First pipe the petals on the
sides as they will lie underneath the other petals. The
two top petals are piped next and should overlap slightly. The fifth petal (at the bottom) is piped on top of the
side petals and is slightly larger than the rest. To make
the stamens and/or pistil, pipe four dots in the centre
(Fig. 69).

Once you have mastered these techniques you will be
able to pipe any variety by simply studying the flower
well.

7. Sweet peas

Stunning effects can be achieved with this flower by
using two different colours of icing in the same bag.

Pipe an almost fully circular petal, fluting it by quickly moving the icing tube up and down while turning the
flower nail (Fig. 70a). The centre vertical petal is piped
next. Hold the tube with the wide end nearly horizontal
to the flower nail. Pipe out the icing and simultaneously
move the tube up and away from you (the icing will

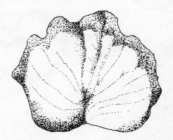

Fig. 70a

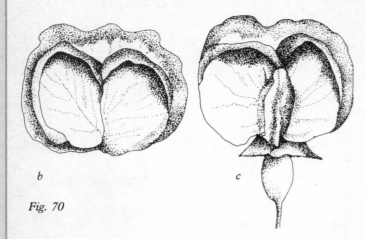

b   *c*

Fig. 70

centre of the flower. It is a good idea to study an actual flower and try to copy the beautiful colour combinations (Fig. 71).

9. Daisies

Although these flowers can be made with the same tube used for the other flowers, an even better result is achieved with a writing tube.

Use a No 1 tube for a small flower and proceed as follows. Make two teardrops opposite each other with their tips touching. Make another two teardrops to form a cross with the first two (Fig. 72a). Fill in the remaining openings with teardrops until you have eight petals (Fig. 72b). Allow them to dry slightly and lightly flatten the teardrops until they assume the shape of petals. Pipe a light green dot in the centre, flatten it and sprinkle a few *nonpareils* on top.

remain in a vertical position). Move the tube slightly towards you to make a groove in the centre. Move it up again and then down (Fig. 70b). Keeping the tube against the flower as if to prevent the icing from running out, pipe while making a slight up and down movement, allowing the icing to bulge out on both sides. Stop piping and lift the tube. Using a No 2 tube and green icing, pipe the calyx and stems (Fig. 70c).

8. Pansies

These cheerful little flowers can be piped by filling an icing bag with two different colours of icing. Pipe two petals slightly more rounded than those of the blossoms and let them overlap slightly (Fig. 71a). Next pipe two rounded petals on both sides, covering about half of the top petals (Fig. 71b). Finally pipe the large base petal. Keeping the tube in a near horizontal position and with its wide end in the centre of the flower, start the circular movement slightly on top of the second petal on the left. Flute the petal while twirling the nail. The petal should just overlap the edge of the second petal on the right (Fig. 71c). Finish the flower by piping a yellow dot in the centre. Leave the flower to dry. Using a fine brush, paint the characteristic lines fanning outwards from the

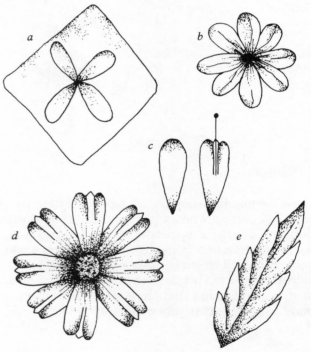

Fig. 72

For a bigger flower it is advisable to make the petals separately. Using a No 2 tube, pipe eight petals in the shape of elongated teardrops. Use a pin to draw a vein down the centre (Fig. 72c). Dry the petals in an apple container in order to bend them slightly. Pipe a light green dot in royal icing on a piece of paper, flatten it and insert the petals into it. Sprinkle yellow *nonpareils* over the dot and allow to dry (Fig. 72d). Pipe the green calyx (Fig. 72e) by using Tala tube No 11 as described in Fig. 56 on p. 43.

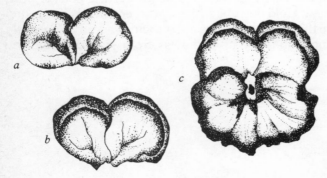

a

c

b

Fig. 71

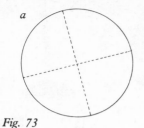

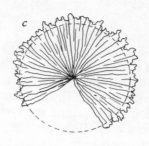

Fig. 73

10. Carnations

These flowers, if made properly, are amongst the prettiest of piped flowers.

Fold a square piece of paper in four. You will only fill three quarters of an imaginary circle with petals (Fig. 73a). Use the petal tube and keep it vertical to pipe an elongated petal. This is really only a slight movement to and fro (Fig. 73b) with a slight "comma" at the top of the petal. Proceed by filling three quarters of the imaginary circle in this way (Fig. 73c). Make another row of shorter petals, halfway over the previous ones. Move the tube closer towards you and pipe another one or two similar rows. The last row of petals should be short and nearly upright. Ensure that you leave a hollow for the calyx.

Fill a bag with green icing, flatten the point and *tear* it off to give it an opening the same size as a No 5 tube. The torn opening should be held in such a way that it forms a notch in the icing. Use this to pipe an elongated petal which will eventually form the calyx. Using a small petal tube filled with green icing, pipe three small petals at the top of the calyx and stroke them with a fine brush so that they blend in with the calyx. Still using the same tube, pipe two small petals at the bottom of the calyx as well as a third petal which slightly overlaps the other two. Pipe the stem at the same time (Fig. 73d).

11. Roses

There are many techniques to make this queen of flowers. The following is an easy method with wonderful results.

Using a No 5 or 6 tube, pipe a cone on a piece of paper to make the heart or centre of the rose (Fig. 74a). Leave to dry for a while. Secure to the flower nail again, using a bit of fresh icing. First cover the tip of the cone with a petal by holding the narrow end of the tube pointing up but against the cone while twirling the nail and wrapping the icing around the cone like a ribbon. Leave a small opening at the top (Fig. 74b). Stop piping and break off the icing against the cone.

Still keeping the tube at a vertical angle, slightly turn the narrow end away from the cone. Pipe again while moving the tube up and down in a semicircle to form a petal on the one side. Pipe a similar petal on the other side, and another two petals opposite the first two, but let these curl slightly outwards (Fig. 74c). The outer petals are next. Move the tube further and further away from the cone and let the petals curl out more (Fig. 74d). Do not pipe too many petals as it gives the rose a clumsy, heavy appearance. The icing should not be too soft either. With green icing pipe a calyx against the bottom petals on the paper. To make a bud, pipe two or three petals. Leave them to dry and, using a No 2 tube, pipe a calyx against the bud.

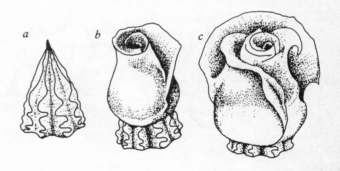

Fig. 74

12. Daffodils and narcissi

These two flowers look very much alike.

To make a daffodil, proceed as follows. Use bright yellow icing and pipe six petals in a circle. They should be slightly larger and more rounded than those of the blossoms and should overlap one another. Ensure that the tube is in a vertical position when piping the last petal so as not to damage the first petal. Pipe the trumpet as follows. Hold the tube with the opening vertical to the flower and the narrow end pointing up. Twirl the nail right round to form the trumpet. Stop piping just before the trumpet is completed so that the two ends meet. The trumpet can also be piped by building it up with a No 1 tube into a circle in the centre of the flower. The first method however, is more successful. Pinch each petal between your thumb and forefinger to form a point (Fig. 75).

The narcissus is smaller than the daffodil and is piped in white instead of yellow icing. White narcissi with yellow trumpets are also popular.

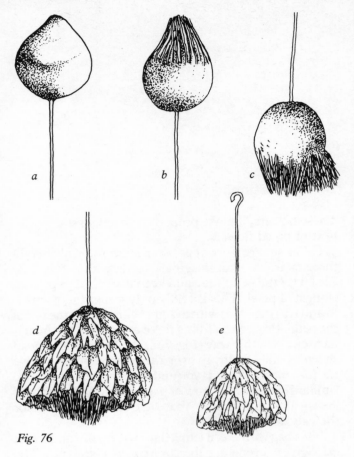

Fig. 76

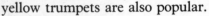

Fig. 75

13. Proteas

Cover a piece of No 24 florist's wire with green florist's adhesive tape and bend it to form a hook at the top end. Mould a cone which is well rounded at the bottom and insert the hook into it (Fig. 76a). Leave it to dry. Fill two icing bags, each with a No 0 or 00 tube, with pale green and pale pink icing respectively. Use them alternately to pipe the stamens (Fig. 76b). Hold the cone horizontally in your left hand and pipe the stamens against the cone towards the top end. Turn it while repeating the procedure.

Repeat the procedure but lower the cone with every layer of stamens you complete so that the stamens stand slightly away from the cone (Fig. 76c). Eventually the cone will be turned upside down. If you want to pipe a large open protea with a diameter of approximately 60 mm, the diameter of the bunch of stamens at the top will be approximately 40 mm. All the dimensions will be less in the case of a smaller protea in bud.

Leave to dry thoroughly. Pipe the petals with pale pink icing from an icing bag with its point cut off and without a tube (see Fig. 76d), to make a ridge in the centre. Keeping the protea upside down, pipe the petals in layers around the cone. The first row of petals should jut out just above the stamens and should stand slightly away from the cone because the cone is upside down. The second layer of petals is piped over the first layer in between the first row of petals. This is followed by a row of shorter petals to cover the entire cone. Bend the end of the wire to form a hook and hang the protea upside down to dry (Fig. 76e).

14. Petunias

In addition to the conventional flower nail, there is another flower nail which is gaining in popularity. It is used for making bell-like flowers such as petunias and consists of two parts: a bell-shaped mould and a small "lid" that fits inside the "bell" (Fig. 77). Put a piece of aluminium foil over the bell, pushing it into the bell with the lid so that the foil takes on the shape of the bell. Pipe the flower inside the bell and remove the foil along with the flower. Leave the flower in the foil to dry.

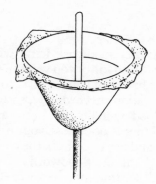

Fig. 77

A petunia is made as follows by means of this nail. Insert a No 18 tube into an icing bag and fill the bag with any shade of pink or mauve icing. Keeping the wide end of the tube facing down and the narrow end facing up, start piping at the bottom of the bell. Move the tube to the top and twirl the flower nail slightly to make quite a large petal. To make the fluted edge, slightly move the tube up and down. Pipe five of these petals. They should slightly overlap each other. Using a No 6 tube, pipe a pale green star in the bottom of the bell and insert a few stamens. Leave to dry. Remove the flower from the foil and pipe a green calyx around the flower by using a paper bag that has been cut to pipe leaves (Fig. 78).

Any bell-shaped flower can be made this way. Study the real flower to see what the petals look like and how they overlap each other.

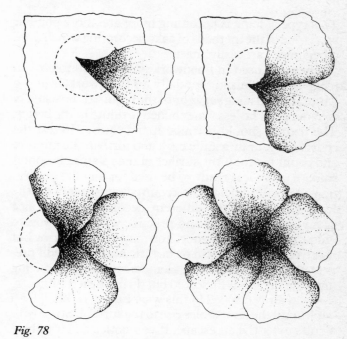

Fig. 78

CHAPTER 9

Creative floodwork

This type of icing is becoming more and more popular and is one of the methods of cake decorating which even a beginner can easily master.

The icing used in floodwork is simply diluted royal icing. If being mixed especially for floodwork, beat egg white and add icing sugar until the required consistency is obtained. The less water added to dilute it, the better. The texture should be smooth and satiny. To test the consistency, draw a knife back and forth in the mixture and count to ten. If the surface of the mixture becomes smooth again it is ready to be used for any flat decoration. We will indicate the required consistency of the icing for each of the different decorations, but once again only experience and practice will enable you to judge the right consistency. You may add flavouring but no glycerine, acetic acid or tartaric acid – this will prevent the icing hardening. Remember to stir the icing until the sugar has dissolved but do not beat it unnecessarily as air is trapped in this way. Leave the icing for a while until the air bubbles rise to the surface. Stir it with a knife to let the air escape. If you notice an air bubble after flooding, immediately prick it with a pin to let the air escape. The icing will flow in smoothly again.

If you live in an area with a high humidity (eg. at the coast) it is advisable to dry floodwork decorations near a heater or a powerful electric light.

1. Loose decorations

Loose decorations for use in an upright or flat position require a firmer consistency than the icing used for flooding flat surfaces such as a plaque or the top of a cake. In addition there are differences in consistency of the icing suitable for various decorations – if the surface needs to be rounded out slightly the icing will be stiffer than when it is used for a flat decoration or a collar.

Place the pattern for the decoration on an even surface, such as a cake board or a tray, and secure it well with adhesive tape or drawing pins. Cover the pattern with a piece of plastic sheeting (the type used to cover books) and secure it. Do not use too much adhesive tape as the ornament might break when you remove it later. Colour the floodwork icing in the required colour(s). Take a little bit of each colour and add sufficient icing sugar until it has the consistency of ordinary royal icing. (When you dip a knife into the mixture and lift it, the point which forms should bend over slowly.) If you

intend diluting the floodwork icing with water you should remove the quantity you want to thicken before adding water. This royal icing is used to trace the outline of the decoration. Accordingly, the colour of each section you flood will be the same as the outline. Another useful hint is not to use your original pattern. Rather trace it and use it to check the completed design while you are doing the floodwork.

Insert a small writing tube (No 1 or 0) into an icing bag and fill it with royal icing of the correct colour. If using a few colours, it is advisable to prepare a number of bags. If you do not have enough tubes, fill a bag with icing without inserting the tube. Prepare a second bag and insert the tube. Cut off the point of the bag containing the icing and slip it into the bag with the tube. When you have finished working with that colour, remove the bag containing the icing and insert the next colour into the bag containing the tube. If some of the previous colour is still in this bag, prepare a new bag for the tube. It is wise to acquire a number of writing tubes because they are often used with different colours.

When the outline of the design is dry, fill a bag (without a tube) with floodwork icing of the required colour. Fold the top over, taking care not to over-fill the bag or it will make a mess, turn the bag upside down and cut off the point. Do not turn the bag over before you have it directly above the portion to be flooded. Always start in the centre of the design to allow the icing to run to the edge. Use a small watercolour paintbrush to spread the icing quickly. Immediately prick any air-bubbles that appear. Do not flood two adjoining surfaces one after the other – the colours might run over the outline. Complete all the sections that do not border on each other and allow them to dry before completing the rest.

Once you have completed the entire decoration, leave it near a heater to dry – not in an oven, as the heat will cause the trapped air to rise to the surface. Do not become impatient – a large decoration can easily take up to three days to dry. Be sure to take this into consideration. Once the decoration is completely dry, carefully loosen the plastic sheeting from the work surface (or cut the plastic sheeting around the decoration loose with a sharp knife), turn the decoration over and peel back the plastic. If the decoration still appears to be a little damp underneath, leave it upside down to dry.

Floodwork can be done directly on to the cake if you first prick the design on the cake, although it is safer to do it separately.

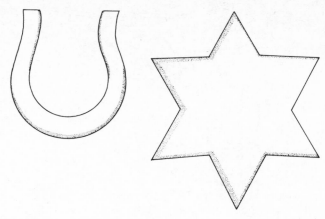

Fig. 79

There are numerous patterns for floodwork at the back of this book. It is a good idea to flood a few simple decorations with left-over royal icing and store them. Next time you ice a cake they might come in handy as a decoration on the sides of the cake (Fig. 79) or even as an upright decoration, for instance numbers. Make more than one decoration of the same kind at a time as you will probably need more than one. Finish the decorations with dots or a border when you have put them on the cake.

2. Animal motifs

These little animals look superb on a cake for a child. Designs can be found in children's colouring-in or picture books. Children are delighted when they discover their favourite animal or cartoon character on a birthday cake. Because children have active imaginations, you need not add minute detail to the figures. Details can be drawn or painted on to the figures after they have dried. We will study the finish of these figures in greater detail in the section on three-dimensional floodwork. Practise making a few of the figures we discuss here (Fig. 80). There are more patterns at the back of this book.

Remember, the decoration for animal figures should not be too runny and should not be flat – it should be slightly rounded. Accentuate limbs by letting them flood first and rounding them out more than the rest of the body. The wing of the swan is made separately and attached to the body afterwards. (You will gradually learn how to give the feathers more detail, although it is not required in this case.)

If you want to arrange the animals in upright positions on the cake (see Fig. 136 on p. 153 and Photograph 38 on p. 118) they should be turned over when they are dry and you should flood them on the other side as well. Alternatively, the pattern can be turned over and you can flood a second animal on the same pattern. When

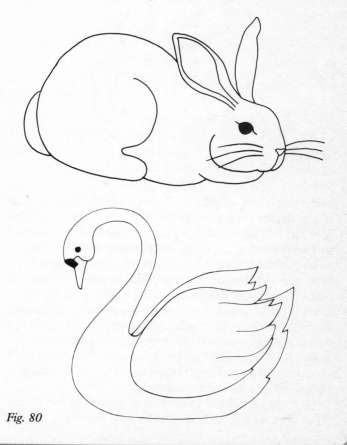

Fig. 80

both are dry they can be joined together with a little icing sugar. Check, however, that they are both the same size. Cover the join with icing and smooth over with a fine paintbrush.

3. Fairies, elves and dwarfs

This is advanced work and requires some experience. We are sure, though, that once you have experimented with this technique you will love it.

The outlines must be done with a No 0 tube; it is therefore worthwhile to mix the correct icing for fine tubes (see p. 17). Once you have decided which figure you want to make, you have to choose the colours. Look at the elf in Fig. 81a. His face and hands will be flesh-

Fig. 81b

Fig. 81a

walnut (without the elf), the mast and the sail. Then make the elf and the outside of the walnut. Join the inside to the outside so that the elf rests inside the walnut. The icing for the outside of the walnut should be quite stiff to accentuate its rough surface.

The ballerina in Fig. 81c is ideal for a cake for a young girl. Remember to flood it at the back as well, but first

coloured, a mix of pale pink and a hint of yellow. You might decide on green for his trousers and cap, red for his shirt and shoes and grey for his beard (add a touch of brown colouring). Colour small quantities of icing *before* you dilute it and be careful not to make it too runny. Pipe the outline of each section in the appropriate colour and then dilute the icing slightly (it must be smooth) to maintain the correct shade for each section. Once again the golden rule of floodwork applies: do not flood two adjacent surfaces until the first one has dried slightly. Finer detail on the figures can be applied at a later stage. You can even make more detailed folds and bulges by painting on shadows.

Proceed as follows to make the walnut in which the elf in Fig. 81b is sailing. First make the inside of the

Fig. 81c

put a toothpick in the leg to keep the figure upright. Because the outline crosses over the toothpick, position the toothpick on the plastic sheeting following the dotted line on the pattern (the full-sized pattern appears at the back of this book) and then pipe the outline. Secure the toothpick to the plastic sheeting with a piece of adhesive tape to prevent it moving. Secure it where the toothpick sticks out at the toe, and not in the pattern itself. Remember to remove the adhesive tape *very* carefully before peeling the plastic sheeting from the figure. Continue flooding all the different parts in their appropriate colours. When flooding the back of the figure, ensure that the hair comes down to the shoulders at the back and that the shoe looks different from the front view. Although it might sound difficult it is actually easy to make these changes. A bit of edible glitter (see p. 14) sprinkled on the dress while it is still damp is most effective. Finish the cake by making an elevated collar around the ballerina. Study the cake in Photograph 43 on p. 123. The pattern for the collar is at the back of this book (Fig. 133 on p. 148).

4. Larger loose decorations

These decorations (Fig. 82) can be used on Christmas or wedding cakes (the full-sized patterns appear at the back of this book on p. 131). Make two horseshoes which can be joined at the top with a ribbon and a bouquet of flowers. Balance them on the cake with the bases splayed out. You should flood them on both sides. The dotted areas represent openings.

Make the bells by first flooding the inside sections. These should be flat. Let the outside section bulge out slightly – the icing should therefore be smooth but not too runny. The ribbon can be varied as well by flooding the different sections to different heights.

Fig. 82

5. Collars

Some of the most interesting objects which can be made by means of this icing technique are collars which are placed on top of a cake. The collar can either rest directly on top of the cake itself or on pillars (cubes of sugar will do). The collar will then be higher than the cake (Fig. 83). The pillars should be positioned so as to be invisible. Finish the outer edge of the collar with extension work, loops or lace points (see Photograph 35 on p. 115).

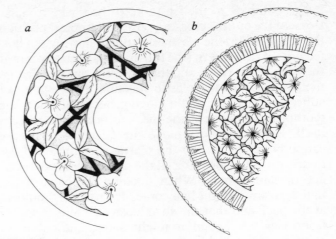

Fig. 84

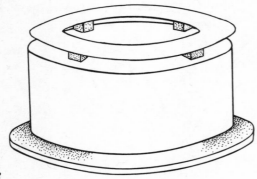

Fig. 83

The collar handles best if it is sturdy and completely dry. A collar resting directly on top of the cake will look more delicate if it is slightly thinner. Other than this, collars are made in exactly the same way as loose decorations on plastic sheeting. Ensure that the plastic sheeting is smooth when placed over the pattern. Do not use clingwrap and do not stretch the plastic. If you do it will contract when you loosen it and break the collar.

Once the collar has dried thoroughly (it can take 24 hours or more) carefully cut the plastic sheeting loose with a small sharp knife if you have used adhesive tape, or remove your drawing pins carefully. Turn the collar over, put it down on a flat surface and carefully peel off the plastic sheeting. If the underside of the collar is not entirely dry, leave it upside down to dry thoroughly.

If you intend balancing the collar on pillars, ensure that you know where to place them. Proceed as follows. Put the pattern on top of the cake and use a pin to prick the spots where the pillars are to be placed, through the pattern, in areas where they will not be visible.

6. Designing collars

When drawing the symmetrical design for a collar, keep in mind that there should be enough points between the different sections to hold the collar together. This is especially necessary in the case of designs which do not

lie flat on the cake but are suspended. If using a symmetrical design, divide the circle (or square or hexagon) in as many even sections as the number of times you want to repeat the design. Also ensure that the design is uniform and that the corners correspond.

In Fig. 84 there are two designs of which you only need repeat one to obtain the full design (the full-sized patterns appear on pp. 132 and 133).

In Fig. 84a you must flood the petals of the pansies separately to prevent them running. The connecting strips (indicated in black) and the borders are done in the same colour as the cake. First do the flowers and leaves, and finally the connecting strips.

Flood the blossoms in Fig. 84b as one round section – the edge of the blossoms should be higher than the centre section. Do not let the petals flow in separately – they will look too heavy. You can create the impression of separate petals by drawing the petals and stamens later. Try creating light and dark shades by letting two separate colours flow in together and mixing them where they join.

Other examples of collars are the candle collar and the horn of plenty collar. Flood the candle collar in one section, excluding the bells. When dry, flood the bells. The collar and the bells can be in the same colour as the cake (including the candle) if you prefer. Also keep in mind the colour of the flowers you will be using. This is a Christmas decoration and traditionally the flowers and candle will be red and the cake and collar white. The bells can be finished with edible glitter or silver-coloured paint. Keep in mind that the section of the design furthest away, for example the inside of the bells and the flame of the candle, must be flooded first to create the correct perspective.

Before positioning the collar on the cake, first prick the open section of the circle on to the cake and decorate it with a scalloped line or dots. The writing should also

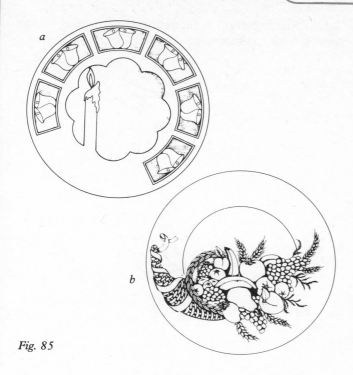

Fig. 85

Another way of drawing the design on to the cake is as follows. Prick the design on to the paper pattern with a pin, put it on top of the cake and rub cocoa over it while taking care not to move the pattern. Remove the paper pattern and paint in the background using a soft paint-brush and powder colouring. Liquid colouring and a good quality brush made from genuine hair can be used for the foreground (eg. blades of grass). Leave to dry. Use brushes Nos 00, 1 and 2 (made from genuine hair) for the floodwork. No outlines are piped.

Colour the royal icing to be used and pour each colour into a separate airtight glass bowl or cover it with clingwrap to prevent a crust forming. Stir each colour thoroughly before using it. Study the design and start with the foreground. Dip a No 1 brush into the icing, scoop up a little icing and start in the centre of the section you want to flood first. Carefully work towards the outline. Remember that the section you flood first should not be too high as this will make the rest of the design too high as well. Use a No 2 brush for larger areas (eg. the dress). Continue building up the design section by section until it appears to be three-dimensional. (The full-sized pattern for Fig. 86a and b appears on p. 136.)

Remember to leave each section you have flooded to dry before commencing with the next section. For the sections of the design which should be raised (the sleeves and shoes) a slightly stiffer icing should be used to make it bulge out more. The figure's head, the rabbits and carrots should also be rounded.

be completed at this stage. (See Fig. 85a on p. 134 for the full-sized pattern and look at Photograph 31 on p. 111.)

For the horn of plenty (Fig. 85b) the entire collar, including the section intersecting the circle, is flooded simultaneously as one large surface. First make another copy of the complete collar so that the horn and fruit can be flooded separately and positioned on top of the collar at a later stage. Once you have flooded the horn you can pipe the basket weave on top of it and then flood the ribbons. (See Fig. 85b on p. 135 for the full-sized pattern.)

7. Three-dimensional floodwork (Australian method)

The surface on which three-dimensional floodwork is done should be bone dry. The texture of the icing should be slightly stiffer than that which is used for ordinary floodwork. If a knife is drawn through the icing, a thread of about 20 mm should hang from the knife – almost like runny honey. The drops that fall from the knife should disappear immediately. If the icing is too thick, a few drops of water can be added by means of a medicine dropper. Stir the icing thoroughly to prevent the surface becoming sugary and stripy.

Choose a suitable design and trace it on to a piece of greaseproof paper. Turn the design over and retrace it with a soft pencil on the other side of the paper. Turn the paper over again so that the original side faces up. Put the pattern on the cake and trace it. The design may be drawn freehand on to the cake.

Fig. 86

Work *towards* the edge but not *against* the outline. Leave to dry. Now proceed as described earlier and work the soft royal icing right up to the outline to define it. This will ensure a smooth, rounded effect. More life can be added to the design by defining detail with a No 00 brush and colouring. The flowers and leaves can be flooded or painted afterwards.

This technique can be combined with painting. The icing used for painting is slightly stiffer than that used for floodwork. Use the flooding method for the smooth sections and paint in the rest by moving the paintbrush up and down, back and forth, or in circles depending on the effect you want to achieve. For Fig. 87 (see p. 136 for the full-sized pattern), proceed as follows: Flood the cap, beak, stork's legs and baby by using the brush, and paint the rest of the stork to achieve a feathered effect. Do all the floodwork and painting according to the numbers on the pattern. To raise the wings holding the baby slightly, leave the first coat of feathers to dry completely before applying the next coat of icing. Work the icing slightly over the edge of the section you have flooded. Draw a line in the centre of each feather and make brush strokes outwards to both sides of the line, slightly towards the tip of the feather, to achieve a feathered look. Study the plaque on Photograph 48 on p. 128.

This three-dimensional flooding has been done in South Africa before, but here it is described as Kinnie saw it done in Australia.

Fig. 87

CHAPTER 10

Crimping and extension work for beginners

1. Crimping

Crimping is a technique initially learnt from the Australians but we have since developed it and achieved extremely high standards.

Technique
Different kinds of crimpers are used (see Fig. 15 on p. 25 for examples). The crimper crimps and stretches the fondant covering of the cake to create different patterns (Fig. 88). The latest wholly South African addition to

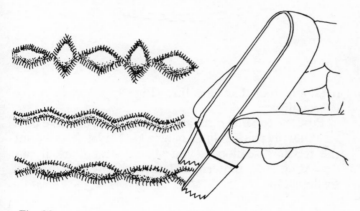

Fig. 88

the crimper range is the Kinnie crimper which is manufactured by the Woolcraft & Hobby Shop in Pietermaritzburg. This crimper has no teeth and is available in different sizes: 20 mm (¾ in), 25 mm (1 in), 40 mm (1½ in), 45 mm (1¾ in) and 50 mm (2 in). It can easily be adapted for ordinary crimping. The use of this most useful piece of equipment is described again in the section on extension work.

An ordinary pair of compasses is indispensible for marking the cake when crimping. It will ensure that the pattern you crimp, either round the edge of the cake or in the centre of the side of the cake, will be even. Crimping should be done with great care and precision. Untidy crimping can spoil the entire appearance of a cake. The cake should be crimped as soon as it has been covered. If the icing is allowed to dry slightly it will form tiny hairline cracks when crimped. The marks left by the serrated edge should be hardly visible. Be careful not to push the crimper too deep into the fondant, and take care not to let the crimper open suddenly – you will

make unsightly marks which are difficult to remove. As is the case with all equipment used for cake decorating, your crimper should be spotlessly clean. Wipe it every now and then, and dust it with cornflour to prevent pieces of fondant from sticking to it. It is a good idea to put an elastic band around the crimper so that the ends can open only 5-6 mm. Insert the crimper 3-4 mm deep into the fondant and crimp gently (it should only close to about 2 mm). Release the pressure while the crimper is still in the fondant until its ends are 5-6 mm apart, and remove it carefully.

It may sound involved but with a little practice it becomes one of the easiest and fastest ways of finishing a cake.

To ensure that the pattern fits around the cake, check how many crimping patterns you still have to do when you are a little way from the starting point again. You can then make the last few crimping patterns closer or further apart. Compasses may be used to determine how many times the width of your crimper fits around the edge of the cake (Fig. 89a and b).

The beginner will find it worthwhile to mark the cake first. Measure the circumference of the cake and decide what size crimper to use. Use compasses for accuracy

a

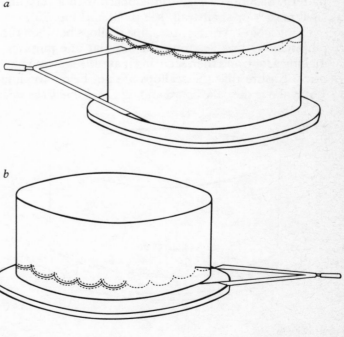

b

Fig. 89

and first press the closed Kinnie crimper ever so slightly against the cake. You are now ready to do the crimping with a serrated crimper – quickly and easily!

2. Extension work

Extension work is another technique that originated in Australia. Although it has been adapted and improved tremendously over the years, the basic principles remain the same.

Technique
A very fine writing tube (No 0 or 00) is used for extension work. First consult Chapter 2 (p. 17) for the correct preparation and mixture of the icing. It is most important that you follow the recipe exactly when making the icing or else you will run into difficulties.

A beginner should not attempt extension work that is done high up against the sides of the cake – the longer the lines, the more easily they will break.

Measure the circumference of the cake and cut out a strip of paper of the same length. Fold it in half and in half again. Repeat until you have the required size of the scallops on which the extension work will be resting. Mark the scallops and cut them out through all the folds of the paper. Mark a line on the sides of the cake approximately 5 mm from the cake board. Position the pattern with the scallops on top of the line and secure with adhesive tape. Clearly mark the outline of the scallops and especially the tops of the arcs on the cake with pinpricks. Use compasses to mark the top of the pattern. Secure the cake to the board with a very fine shell border or snailstrail (see p. 40 and Fig. 90).

Using a No 1 writing tube, pipe scallops between the pinpricks by first securing the icing at one pinprick, making a loop and then securing it at the following pinprick. Ensure that the scallops are not below the line 5 mm above the cake board and that *they touch the side*

of the cake. Leave each row to dry thoroughly before piping the following row directly against the previous one. Pipe four or five lines, each slightly shorter than the preceding one, until you are satisfied that the little "platform" of scallops stands away from the cake far enough (approximately 5 mm) and that it makes an evenly scalloped line. When the cake is held at eye-level,

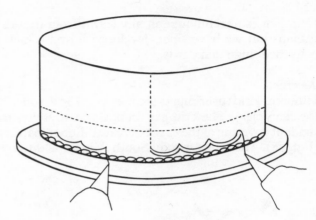

Fig. 91

it should look like one line (Fig. 91). Leave to dry thoroughly.

Pipe the top line right around the cake, or make dots all along the pricked line, using a No 1 tube. If you want the top line scalloped, you should first mark it out according to a pattern and then follow the marked scallops only.

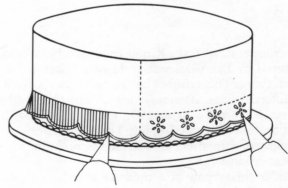

Fig. 92

With the cake at eye-level and using a No 0 or 00 tube, pipe the vertical lines. Hold the edge of the tube against the top line, apply even pressure and move the tube slightly outwards, down and back again to secure the icing to the scalloped platform. This prevents one from accidentally touching and damaging the previous line. The lines should be so close together that there is no room between them for another line. Proceed in this way right around the cake (Fig. 92).

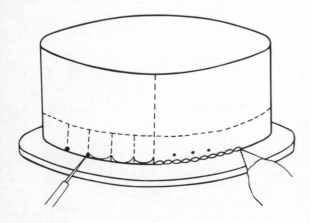

Fig. 90

Leave all the lines to dry completely and finish them neatly. This can be done in a variety of ways: a row of lace points can be secured to the top edge as well as loops to the bottom line (Fig. 93).

If embroidery is to be done underneath the extension work, this should be done *before* making the platforms. Even other embroidery work on the sides of the cake should preferably be done before building the platforms. It is most important that the extension work does not touch the cake board as it will easily break if the board is moved.

When doing extension work for the first time, it might be helpful to tilt the cake *slightly*, so that the top of the cake is closer to you than the bottom. The vertical lines will hang away from the cake. It is preferable to use a cake board not much bigger than the cake. The platforms should not jut out over the edge of the board. To maintain balance the cake, as well as its original board, can be transferred to a larger board once the extension work has been completed. This larger cake board should then be decorated to blend in with the rest of the work.

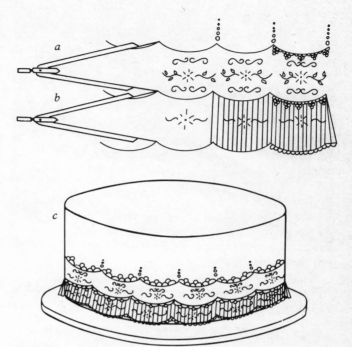

Fig. 94

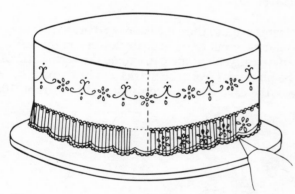

Fig. 93

3. Combining crimping and extension work

Using the Kinnie crimper for extension work
Pipe a row of shells or a snailstrail along the bottom of the cake to secure it to the board. Measure the circumference of the cake and decide on the size of the scallops. Choose a Kinnie crimper with the same or nearly the same measurement as the scallops. Mark a line 5 mm above the board on the side of the cake. Crimp the scallops along this line with the Kinnie crimper and make the necessary adjustments.

Using compasses, mark the top line from where you intend doing the extension work right around the cake. Mark it from the top of the scallops (Fig. 94a). With the same Kinnie crimper used for the bottom scallops, gently crimp the design opposite the bottom scallops. If

making embroidery on the sides of the cake as well, mark another row of scallops with your compasses and Kinnie crimper, approximately 7-8 mm above the first line. This will provide you with a line along which you can pipe dots or make lace points (Fig. 94b). Fig. 94c illustrates the finished result of the decoration we have just described.

Put an elastic band around a Kinnie crimper to prevent the ends from moving apart more than 5-6 mm. Insert the crimper approximately 5 mm deep into the fondant on the design that has been marked and close the crimper until the crimping ends are approximately 2 mm apart. Keeping it in this position, carefully draw out 2 mm of fondant to form a protruding scallop. (Take care not to pinch it off entirely.) Reduce the pressure

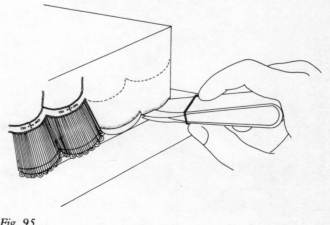

Fig. 95

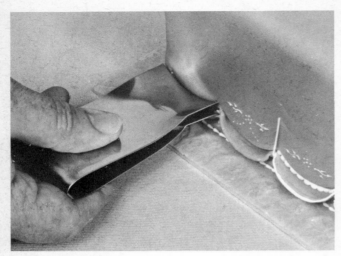

Photograph 10a

and remove the crimper (see Photograph 10a and Fig. 95 on p. 63).

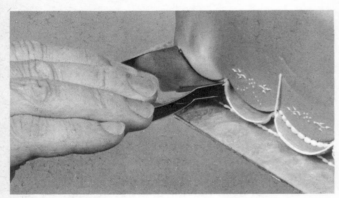

Photograph 10b

Dust the crimper with a little cornflour, shake off any excess and carefully extend the scallop approximately another 1 mm (Photograph 10b). Repeat the last step

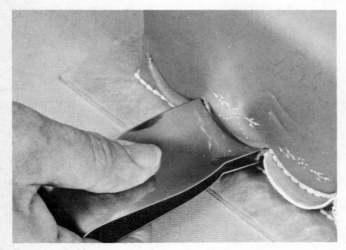

Photograph 10c

once more – the scalloped platform should be about 4–5 mm wide (Photograph 10c). Finish the platforms with a damp paintbrush.

Using a No 1 tube, build up any platforms that are not completely rounded (Photograph 10d). When all the

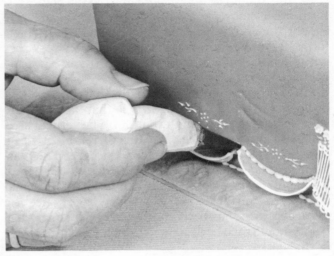

Photograph 10d

platforms around the cake have been drawn out, pipe a row of dots or put a few delicate flowers on the inside to finish it neatly. Now you can extend the vertical threads to the platforms from the marks you have made on the side of the cake with the compasses (Photograph 10e).

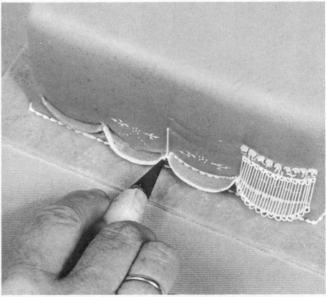

Photograph 10e

Note: This technique should be applied immediately after covering the cake while the fondant is still quite soft.

4. Combining crimping and ribbon inserts

Well-finished crimping alone will make a cake look fine. When it is combined with embroidery and ribbon inserts the effect is magnificent. As in the case of crimping, the ribbon should be inserted while the fondant is still soft. Use good quality florist's ribbon or roll out modelling paste very thinly and use this to make pieces of ribbon. The latter technique might be a bit advanced for a beginner – it should, however, always be the cake decorator's ideal to make everything on the cake edible.

Design the entire cake beforehand. Decide how far apart you want to do the crimping and determine the width of the ribbon accordingly. In Fig. 96 you will notice that the cake board is also covered in fondant and that crimping has been done along the top edge of the cake as well as on the edge of the board. (This was done first, as described on p. 61.) Using the compasses, mark against the side of the cake exactly where you want to "thread" the ribbon. Then mark where the ribbon is to be inserted. You therefore make two marks – the ribbon is secured in such a way that it looks as if it has been threaded in and out. The distance between the marks where the two ends of the ribbon are inserted and the distance between the two pieces of ribbon do not necessarily have to be the same. Calculate accurately how it will fit around the circumference of the cake. The pieces of ribbon should be approximately 6 mm longer than the distance between the cuts into which they will be inserted on both sides. They should be inserted deep enough into the fondant to prevent them slipping out.

Make a fairly deep vertical cut at the marks where the ribbon is to be inserted. Curl the ribbon slightly by pulling it against the side of a knife blade and dab a little egg

Fig. 97

your compasses and make a mark 5 mm above and below the line. Using a crimper of your choice, make scallops or other shapes along the top line. Turn the crimper round and repeat the pattern on the bottom line, directly opposite the pattern on the top line. Make small holes in the centre line with a thin knitting needle directly opposite the ends of the scallops. Dab each hole with a little egg white, using a small brush. Anchor the ribbon in one of the holes with the knitting needle so that the ribbon just adheres to the hole and there is a small hole in the ribbon. Lightly hold the ribbon in a slightly curved position and insert it into the following hole by using the knitting needle. Proceed in this manner until the entire ribbon has been threaded. Pipe tiny dots of royal icing into the holes in the ribbon and place forget-me-nots on them.

Photograph 11

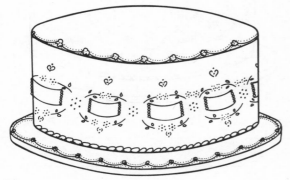

Fig. 96

white on the ends. Use tweezers to insert the two ends into the grooves you have just made (see Fig. 55 and Photograph 8 on p. 42 and Photograph 11).

You can thread the ribbon without cutting it into sections (Fig. 97). Use a ribbon approximately 3 mm wide and one and a half times the circumference of the cake. Mark the centre line of the side of the cake with

A third method of decorating a cake with ribbon is to make the cuts a little closer together, still leaving a gap between them. Take small pieces of ribbon, fold them in half, dab a bit of egg white on the ends and insert both ends in the grooves at the same time by using tweezers (see Photograph 12 on p. 66). It will be easier to "thread" the ribbon if you can tilt the cake at an angle. If your turntable cannot tilt, simply slide a piece of foam rubber, approximately 10 mm thick, underneath the cake to prevent it slipping.

Photograph 12

5. Combining crimping with filigree and embroidery

When combining crimping with filigree or embroidery, it is most important that the design of the crimping should be accurately calculated and that both the embroidery design and the lace points fit in. (The pattern can be cut in two different ways – see Fig. 98.)

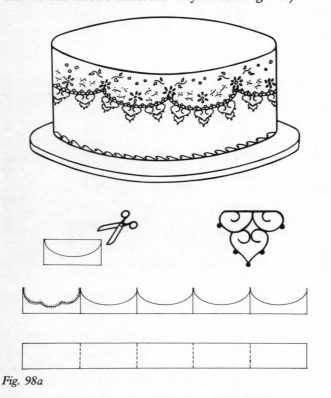

Fig. 98a

Fig. 98a: Measure the circumference of the cake exactly – do not guess. Fold, mark and cut the pattern. Use the compasses to mark the place where you want to do the crimping. Place the pattern on the cake, secure it with adhesive tape and prick the pattern on to the cake.

Alternatively use a dressmaker's wheel to mark it. Crimp the design evenly along the line. Ensure that the lace points are the correct size to fit in with the crimping. If not, make the necessary adjustments.

Fig. 98b

Fig. 98b: Decide in advance where on the cake you want the embroidery and prick the pattern on to the cake in as much detail as possible. Then secure the pattern to the cake board below the area where you are going to do the embroidery as a reference point while working. (Only a very experienced cake decorator will attempt freehand embroidery.) If using lace points as well, make a few extra in case some of them break. Remember to finish the crimping with dots or lines if not using lace points.

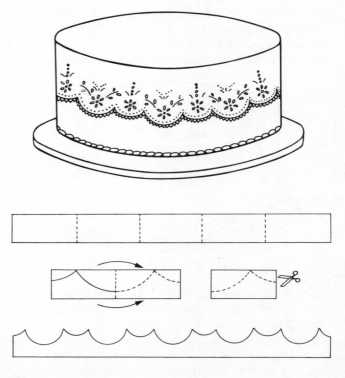

Fig. 98c

Fig. 98c: Proceed as explained in Fig. 98a but fold the paper once more after folding it into five equal sections. Cut out the pattern by following the illustration in Fig. 98c. The pattern can be adapted in many ways – just ensure that it is accurate and that the paper is long enough to go right around the cake.

In the case of a square cake, only measure one side (Fig. 98d) or a quarter of the full length. Remember that the corners are only decorated with half the design. This is not done, however, if the complete design fits each side, in which case you should ensure that the designs match up at the corners. The same goes for hexagonal and octagonal cakes. Proceed to decorate the cake according to taste.

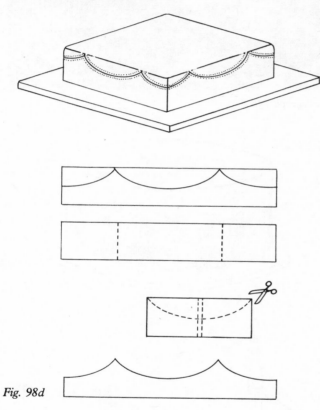

Fig. 98d

6. Crimping variations

There are very many crimping variations. It is important always to use compasses to ensure accuracy and use the same crimper throughout. Here are a few suggestions:

Fig. 99a, b, c, d, e: Use the Kinnie crimper to make platforms and decorate the cake quickly and accurately in a variety of ways.

Designs can be made by pressing the ends of the Kinnie crimper together and lightly pressing it against the cake. In Fig. 99a, b and c the same design, a perfect triangle with curved lines, is used in different ways.

Ensure that the width of your Kinnie crimper fits in with the circumference of the cake – adjust the marks if necessary. With a pair of compasses, mark a horizontal line on which to make the design and then lightly mark the horizontal scallops with the closed crimper. Draw an imaginary vertical line by positioning the compasses across the width of the scallop (Fig. 99a1) and then placing one end in the centre of the scallop. Place the compasses in a vertical position and mark the spot (Fig. 99a2). You can now easily mark the two sides of the triangle very lightly with the Kinnie crimper. This design has endless possibilities.

In Fig. 99a the design was lightly crimped with a serrated crimper and then finished. Embroidery was done inside the triangles, but you can pipe dots instead.

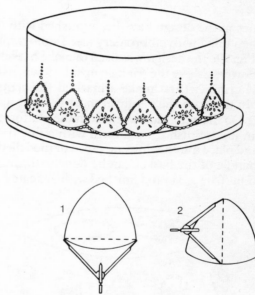

Fig. 99a

In Fig. 99b the lower scallops can be extended with a Kinnie crimper. Alternatively you can build up a platform in the traditional manner (see p. 62) and then do extension work across the triangle with possibly a bit of embroidery underneath. In the other half of Fig. 99b

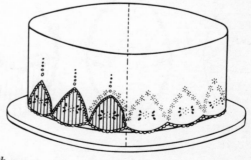

Fig. 99b

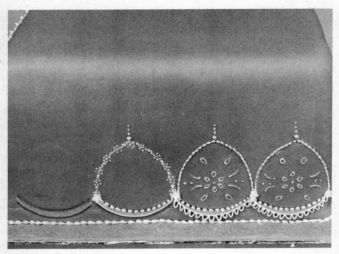

Photograph 13a

(Use a No 1 or 0 tube.) See Photograph 42 on p. 122 and Photograph 13b for more variations.

Another interesting way of making a design with the

Photograph 13b

the lines of the design have been finished with flowers and then filled with embroidery (see Photograph 13a).

In Fig. 99c the design was used to make baskets filled with flowers. Make the triangle upside down, using the Kinnie crimper (first make a mark at the centre bottom). In this case the platform must be built up *in the centre.* Do the extension work from the platform to the bottom lines, finish the platform with a fine thread or dots and place minute flowers (piped or modelled) on it. The handle of the basket can be done with the roping technique (see p. 31) and finished with delicate ribbons.

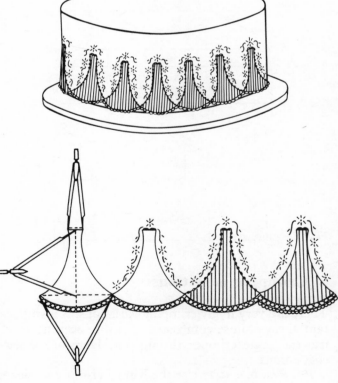

Fig. 99d

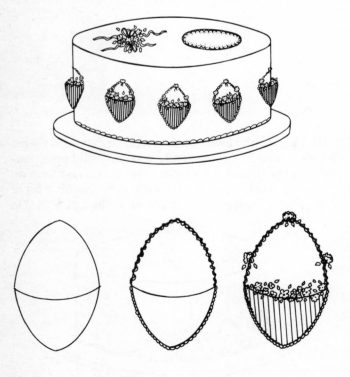

Fig. 99c

Kinnie crimper is illustrated in Fig. 99d and e. Proceed exactly as you would for Fig. 99a but turn the Kinnie crimper round with the curve on the inside. Use compasses to draw a horizontal line and determine the imaginary vertical line. Leave a gap of approximately 3 mm at the top on either side of the imaginary centre line. Finish the design with embroidery or any decoration according to taste (see Photograph 14.)

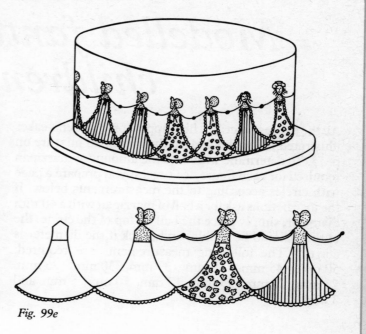

Fig. 99e

Photograph 14

CHAPTER 11

Modelled fantasy figures for children's cakes

All the figures described here appear on children's cakes illustrated in this book. Use the marzipan mixture on p. 15. To determine with ease the amount of marzipan required for each figure, we suggest you prepare a page with circles according to the measurements below. If the instructions ask for a ball of marzipan with a 40 mm diameter, simply place the ball on top of the circle (the outline should be visible) and check if the diameter is correct. The following measurements are required: 50 mm, 45 mm, 35 mm, 33 mm, 30 mm, 25 mm, 23 mm, 20 mm, 15 mm, 12 mm, 10 mm, 5 mm and 3 mm.

1. The witch *(Fig. 100)*

Requirements
brown royal icing
brown, black, red and flesh-coloured marzipan
two toothpicks
egg white or gum acacia (to attach the pieces if the marzipan is too dry)
white fondant

Method
Base: Shape a black marzipan ball with a 50 mm diameter to form the base (a).
Shoes: Slightly flatten two black marzipan balls with a 15 mm diameter each. Secure them to the base. The points of the shoes should be quite long so that they can show from underneath the dress. Bend them slightly upwards and shape them into points.
Dress: Roll out a black marzipan ball with a 50 mm diameter and cut out a dress according to the pattern at the back of the book. Cut out a 6 mm wedge and place it on top of the base and shoes with the points of the shoes showing. Use a sharp-pointed skewer to make a hollow into which the head and neck can fit. Insert a toothpick into the base, allowing 10 mm to protrude (c).

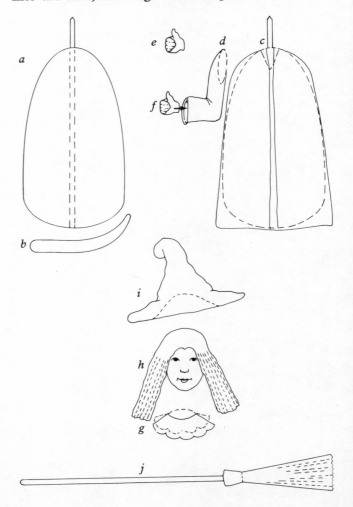

Fig. 100

Arm (sleeve):   Roll a ball of black marzipan with a 15 mm diameter into a sausage. Shape the arm and, using a skewer with a rounded end, make a hole into which the hand can fit. Flatten the upper arm slightly to join the body neatly and make one or two grooves at the elbow to bend the arm (d).

Hand: For each hand, roll a ball of flesh-coloured marzipan with a 10 mm diameter into a cone. Flatten the wide end and carve out a thumb and fingers (e). Paint a little egg white on the other end and insert the hand into the arm (f). Position the arms, secure with a little egg white or gum acacia and bend. It should look as if the witch were holding the broom.

Collar: Shape a flesh-coloured ball of marzipan into a round collar (g). Place it over the upper arms to cover the joins.

Head: Shape a ball of flesh-coloured marzipan with a 25 mm diameter into a head and chin. Make hollows for the eyes. Cut out the mouth with a small pair of scissors or make a groove with a small knife. Use a small piece of red marzipan for the lips. Shape a nose from a ball of flesh-coloured marzipan with a 3 mm diameter and secure it with egg white or gum acacia. Fashion two nostrils with a toothpick (h).

Neck: Slightly flatten a ball of flesh-coloured marzipan with a 5 mm diameter and place it on top of the toothpick protruding from the base. Coat the neck in a little egg white and position the head. Using white fondant, roll two small balls and flatten them; paint eyes on them, coat the backs with a little egg white and secure them to the head. Paint on the face and cheeks.

Hat: Shape a sharp-pointed hat from a ball of black marzipan with a 23 mm diameter. Hollow it out with a small ball tool (i).

Hair: Pipe shoulder-length hair with a No 5 star tube and brown icing. Put the hat on the head while the icing is still soft.

Broom: Roll a ball of brown marzipan with a 12 mm diameter into a cone. Flatten the wide end and cut it into strips. Insert a toothpick at the other end (j) and put the broom into the witch's hand.

2. Dwarf *(Fig. 101)*

Requirements
brightly coloured marzipan for clothes
flesh-coloured marzipan
white and grey royal icing
toothpicks

Method
Body and legs (including the trousers):   Roll a ball of red marzipan with a 50 mm diameter into a flat sausage. Halve two thirds of the sausage (a). Roll it lightly be-

Fig. 101

tween your thumb and forefinger (thinner at the ankles where the trousers fit into the shoes) and shape the upper body. Position the body in a sitting position with the legs either crossed or straight on a rock made of coloured marzipan (c). Remember to make a kneecap. Insert a toothpick into each leg if the dwarf is to stand (b).

Shoes: Shape two pointed shoes from two balls of green marzipan with a 15 mm diameter. Hollow them

Fig. 101

Photograph 15

out with a small ball tool, cut out a V on both sides, and neatly finish by hand. Insert the legs into the shoes (d). Insert a toothpick at the top of the body, allowing 10 mm to protrude.

Jacket: Cut a circle with a 100 mm diameter from a rolled-out ball of yellow marzipan with a 30 mm diameter. Cut out one quarter, cut out Vs right round the circle (e) and place it around the body. Make four small holes at the front on both sides of the seam, and insert four small red balls of marzipan for the buttons. Proceed exactly as you would for the witch, remembering that the arms and collar must be the same colour as the jacket. The pointed hat is slightly smaller (20 mm diameter) and must be the same colour as the shoes.

Ears: For each pointed ear, shape a ball of flesh-coloured marzipan with a 10 mm diameter and secure to the head (f). Pipe the hair and the beard to the head with a No 5 star tube and grey royal icing. Finish neatly with a fine brush and put the hat on the head (g).

The facial expression can be altered by shaping the mouth in various ways. The beard may be omitted. The dwarfs can be dressed in different colours and can be placed in different positions (Photograph 15).

3. Toadstool *(Fig. 102)*

Requirements
red and neutral marzipan
a small quantity of white royal icing or fondant

Method
Stem: Roll a ball of marzipan with a 15 mm diameter into a fat sausage. Flatten the bottom end so that the toadstool can stand (a).

Cap: Shape a ball of red marzipan with a 15 mm diameter as illustrated in (b). Hollow it out with a small ball tool and continue shaping with your fingers. Pipe small dots of white royal icing on top and flatten them with your finger. Alternatively make small discs from white fondant and secure to the toadstool. Paint a little gum acacia on the top of the stem and secure the head (c). Make toadstools of different sizes.

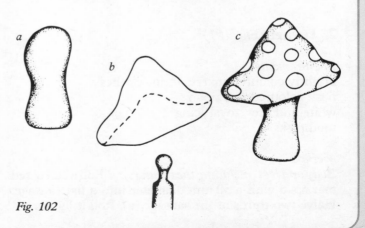

Fig. 102

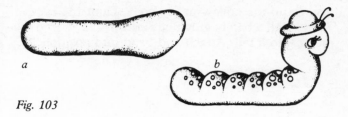

Fig. 103

4. Worm *(Fig. 103)*

Requirements
green marzipan
a few pieces of thin stamen
piece of yellow or pink marzipan for the hat
a small quantity of royal icing

Method
Roll a ball of green marzipan with a 15 mm diameter into a fat sausage. It should be fatter at the head. Shape according to (a), make hollows for the eyes and pipe white icing into them. Support the head and tail slightly and leave to dry. Shape a hat and position on top of the head. Insert the feelers and paint the eyes (b).

5. Duck *(Fig. 104)*

Requirements
yellow marzipan
a small piece of orange marzipan
a small quantity of white royal icing

Fig. 104

Method
Body: Roll a piece of yellow marzipan into a ball with a 23 mm diameter and shape as in (a). Make a hollow for the head. Cut the wingtips with a pair of scissors and form the ends to look like feathers.
Beak: Roll a ball of orange marzipan with a 12 mm diameter into a sausage, flatten it and give it a sharp-pointed end. Position in front of the hollow for the head and attach it firmly (b).
Head: Make hollows for the eyes in a ball of yellow marzipan with a 10 mm diameter. Position the head on the body. Pipe a little royal icing into the hollows and leave to dry.
Feet: Roll a ball of orange marzipan with a 12 mm diameter into a small sausage. Flatten, make the toes (c) and position the duck on top (d). Paint the eyes.

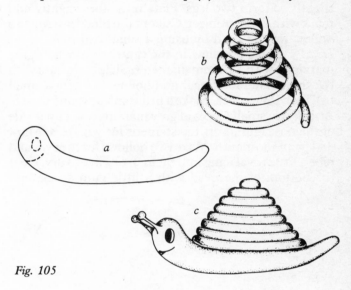

Fig. 105

6. Snail *(Fig. 105)*

Requirements
light brown marzipan
a small quantity of royal icing
2 pieces of stamen

Method
Body: Roll a ball of light brown marzipan with a 15 mm diameter into a small sausage. It should be slightly rounded at one end (head) and thinner at the other (tail). Cut out the mouth and make hollows for the eyes (a). Pipe a little royal icing into the hollows and leave to dry. Insert two stamens for feelers above the eyes and paint the eyes. Support the head and tail slightly.
Shell: Roll a ball of light brown marzipan into a small sausage approximately 180 mm long and twist into a spiral (b). Brush the sides of the sausage lightly with a bit of gum arabic to make it easier to roll the spiral and to make the coils stick. Position on top of the body (c). The shell can be done in a darker colour.

7. Cat (Fig. 106)

Requirements
grey marzipan
a small quantity of white royal icing
a few stamens
a small quantity of pink marzipan
gum acacia

Method
Body: Roll a ball of grey marzipan with a 30 mm diameter into a long pear shape. Make a 20 mm cut on the front (a) with a small sharp knife, and separate slightly to form two legs. Flatten the toes slightly and mark with a sharp object. Cut out the hind legs. Make a hollow for the head by using a small ball tool.
Head: Make a hollow in the centre of a ball of grey marzipan with a 20 mm diameter. Shape two ears with the thumb and forefinger and hollow out with a small ball tool. Roll a neck. Make a little pink nose and attach. Attach two small pieces of grey marzipan on either side of the nose and insert the stamens for whiskers. Mark and paint the mouth. Make two hollows for the eyes and pipe a little royal icing into them (b). Leave to dry. Coat the bottom of the head with a little gum acacia and

insert into the hollow in the body. Paint the eyes.
Tail: Roll a ball of grey marzipan with a 12 mm diameter into a tail. Attach and bend into position (c).

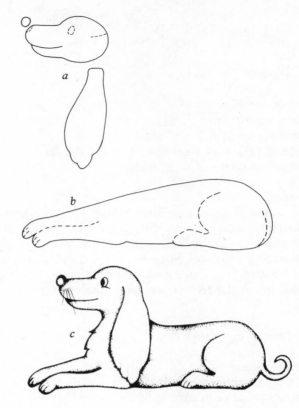

Fig. 107

8. Dog (Fig. 107)

Requirements
brown marzipan
a small quantity of royal icing
a few stamens

Method
Body: Using a ball of brown marzipan with a 35 mm diameter, proceed exactly as for the cat. Cut out a tail, (b) roll into a slight sausage, shape and bend.
Head: Shape a ball of brown marzipan with a 23 mm diameter according to (a). Mark the mouth, make a hollow at the front for the nose and insert a small dark brown ball. Make hollows for the eyes and cut grooves on both sides of the head to insert the ears. Pipe a little royal icing into the hollows for the eyes and leave to dry. Insert a few stamens for the whiskers. Paint dots above the whiskers and eyes.
Ears: For each ear, roll a ball of brown marzipan with a 12 mm diameter into a pear shape and flatten. Make a few notches with a toothpick and insert the back of the ears into the grooves on both sides of the head (c).

Fig. 106

9. Tortoise *(Fig. 108)*

Requirements
light brown marzipan
dark brown marzipan
a small quantity of royal icing
liquid vegetable colouring

Method
Head and tail: Shape the face, using a ball of light brown marzipan with a 20 mm diameter. Cut out the mouth at the bottom and make hollows for the eyes with a small ball tool.
Legs: Roll a ball of light brown marzipan with a 20 mm diameter into two sausages. Flatten the ends slightly, mark the toes (b) and place horizontally across the head and tail section. Lift the head slightly and sup-port with a piece of foam rubber.
Body: Roll a ball of light brown marzipan with a 25 mm diameter into an egg shape and flatten slightly – especially on the sides. Lay it over the legs with the head and tail protruding (c). This gives the body an attractively curved shape.
Shell: Roll a ball of dark brown marzipan with a 30 mm diameter into an egg shape. Finish shaping it with your fingers. Make circles on the shell with a small biscuit cutter or lid and scallop the edge (d). Hollow out the shell to cover the curved body and place into posi-tion. Pipe a little white royal icing into the hollows for the eyes. Leave to dry. Paint the eyes and the pattern on the shell with liquid vegetable colouring.
Model a hat, insert a stamen with a flower into the hat and put it on the tortoise's head (e).

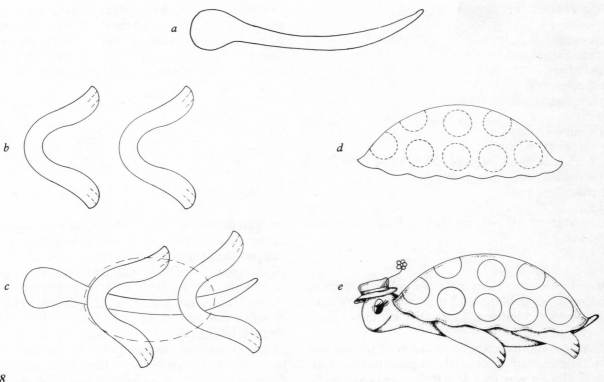

Fig. 108

CHAPTER 12

Simple hand-modelled flowers

Students who attend cake decorating classes are always keen to get started on the modelling of flowers. We have purposely left it till last because this book aims to provide a solid foundation on which to build, for someone who intends becoming a good cake decorator – and this means, primarily, tubework. One often sees at shows cakes with beautifully modelled flowers but scant and even untidy tubework. We hope you have discovered the appeal of tubework in the preceding chapters.

1. Dog roses

Requirements
1 ml maize meal
1 ml gelatine
powder colouring
very thin cotton thread (No 50)
fuse wire
florist's adhesive tape
egg white or gum acacia
florist's wire, covered (Nos 24, 26 and 28)
pink modelling paste (see p. 19)
green modelling paste
cornflour
a small quantity of pale yellow or lemon-coloured
  royal icing

Method
Pollen and stamens: First make the pollen by mixing the maize meal, gelatine and (yellow or yellow and brown) powder colouring. Store in a container with a lid.

To make the stamens, wrap cotton thread around two fingers 20 times. Remove from the fingers and twist into a figure 8. Hook a very thin wire (fuse wire) around the centre of the 8 and, keeping the loops together, twist the fuse ends until tight. Repeat the process – you will now have four loops that neatly fit into each other. Twist the wires together, cover with green florist's adhesive tape, tidy them and cut off evenly. Fan out the threads and gradually cut them shorter towards the centre so that they are not all the same length. Ensure that the length of the stamens is correct in relation to the size of the rose you intend making (Fig. 109a).

Coat the ends of the stamens with egg white or gum acacia and insert them into the prepared pollen. Secure to the florist's wire with florist's adhesive tape.
Loose petals: Make five loose petals by rolling out pink modelling paste with a small metal rolling-pin until the paste is very thin. Cut out the petals with a small cutter. If you do not have a cutter, shape a little paste with your fingers according to the pattern in Fig. 109b. Roll the edge with the rolling-pin until it is extremely thin and

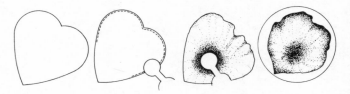

Fig. 109b

cut into the correct shape with a pair of scissors. Cover each petal with plastic to prevent it from drying out. Put one petal at a time in the palm of your hand and roll the edges again with a small ball tool. Half of the rounded end should rest on the petal and the other half on the palm of your hand. In this way only the edge of the petal is rolled out very thinly and fluted. Make the petal slightly hollow in the centre and lay it over a large marble or table tennis ball to dry. Proceed in this manner until all five petals have been completed.
Rose-leaf: Place two pieces of modelling paste (pale green and dark green) on top of each other and roll out (thinner towards the edge than in the centre). Cut out

Fig. 109a

three leaves, one large and two small, ensuring that the front end of the cutter is on the thin part. Make a hook at one end of the covered florist's wire (No 26 or 28) and flatten it. (It should be small and neat to prevent damage to the leaf.) Pinch the leaf all along its edge to make it even thinner. (While finishing one leaf, ensure that the other two are covered with a piece of thin plastic.) Insert the wire (hooked end first) into approximately one third of the leaf and press lightly to secure it (Fig. 109c).

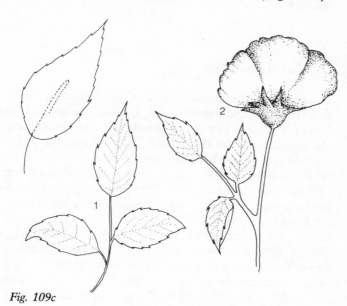

Fig. 109c

Press the leaf on to the back of a real rose-leaf with prominent veins to get a clear impression of the veins. A plastic leaf can be used instead. Crumple a piece of waxed paper or use a small piece of foam rubber, bend the leaf slightly and leave to dry on top of the crumpled paper. (Never dry the leaf flat – it will look stiff and unnatural.) Using a dry paintbrush, paint different shades of green and brown powder colouring on the surface of the leaf. For autumn colours a touch of red or yellow colouring can also be used. Boil some water in a kettle and quickly pass the leaf through the steam; this will give the leaf a very natural appearance.

Complete the spray of leaves by securing the wires of two small leaves to the wire of the large leaf with florist's adhesive tape. The two smaller leaves should be placed opposite each other, slightly below the larger leaf (Fig. 109c1).

Calyx: Roll out the green modelling paste very thinly. Using a cutter of which the size is in relation to the flower, cut out the whole calyx as one piece in the shape of a star. If you do not have a cutter, draw a star-shaped pattern and cut out the calyx with a sharp knife (Fig. 109c2 and 110e on p. 78). Sift a little cornflour into the palm of your hand (this will look like pollen) and roll the edges of the leaves with a small ball tool to make them

even thinner. Draw the instrument from the tip of the leaf to its centre to curl the leaf slightly.

Dog rose: Method 1

Roll out a piece of pink paste very thin and, using a blossom cutter, cut out a small blossom with a 10 mm diameter (or cut it out according to the pattern in Fig. 110a). Put a small piece of waxed paper in the hollow of an apple tray and place the blossom on top. The blossom will prevent the petals from sliding around. Paint with egg white or water. Attach the petals to the blossom according to the illustration (Fig. 110b and c).

The petals should be dry; if not, support them with cotton wool. Make a hole in the centre of the flower and the container through which to pass the stamens. Leave to dry.

Make the calyx as described above and coat it with egg white or water. Carefully remove the flower from the container, turn it over and position the calyx so that each sepal corresponds with a petal. Return the flower to the container. Insert the wire with the stamens through the hole in the flower, the calyx and the container until the stamens are lying neatly against the petals. Put the container on top of an empty jar with the wire hanging inside the jar (Fig. 110d). Pipe a dot of pale yellow or lemon-coloured royal icing in the centre of the stamens. Leave to dry.

Roll some green paste into a cone and insert the wire

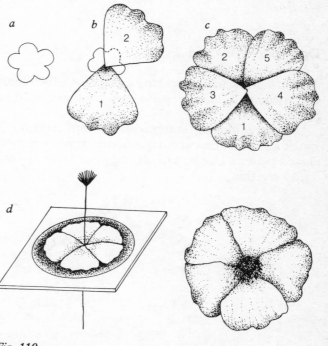

Fig. 110

Photograph 16

through that as well. Coat the top with egg white and attach the cone by pressing it against the calyx to form the ovary (Fig. 110e). (See Photograph 16).

Fig. 110e

Dog rose: Method 2

This is a quick way of making a dog rose which looks very striking if done properly (see Photograph 46 on p. 126).

Use a large blossom cutter with a 50 mm diameter. If you do not have one, cut out the modelling paste according to a pattern. Use pink modelling paste and roll it out until very thin.

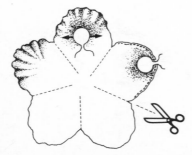

Fig. 110f

Cut the rose petals according to Fig. 110f. Lay the petals in the palm of your hand and proceed as for the first method, except that the petals have to be rolled across their width as well to overlap one another. Place the flower in the centre of an apple container and support the petals with cotton wool.

It is unnecessary to make an extra blossom for this flower or to use a marble; otherwise proceed according to the first method. The dog rose can be made in different sizes.

2. Standard rose

Flower: Decide on the colour of the roses and mix a few shades of the same colour. Use the darker shades first. The darker rose petals should be on the inside and the lighter ones on the outside. Keep a piece of polystyrene handy in which to insert the stems of the roses while they are drying. Make a hook at the end of a piece of covered florist's wire (No 24 for small roses and No 18 for large ones – see Fig. 111a). Shape a cone around the hook and leave to dry (Fig. 111b and c). Make quite a few so that you can work on a few roses simultaneously. Obviously you will make very small cones for the small roses. The first petal of a small rose differs from that of a large rose in that it is elongated with a very thinly rolled out edge. Coat the petal with egg white and wrap it around the cone to cover its tip. (It will go round the cone a few times.) Roll out the modelling paste for the large rose quite thinly. To make the petal, use a petal cutter or cut it freehand. Roll the top of the petal until it is very thin with a small metal rolling-pin. Coat the cone with egg white or water and wrap the petal around the cone. There should be a small opening at the top, but the tip of the cone should not be visible (Fig. 111d).

Roll out the remaining two petals until very thin and secure them on either side of the cone, allowing them to overlap slightly. Although they overlap, they should not be curled (Fig. 111e). Roll out some more petals, flute their edges slightly and wrap them around the cone in a natural way. In some instances, curl them slightly with a toothpick. When the toothpick is removed they will return to their original position but a natural curl will remain (Fig. 111f).

It is a good idea to copy a real rose. No two roses are identical. One of the most important things to remember is that the tops of the petals should be extremely thin and that they should only be secured at their base so that they stand away partially from the rest of the flower. Support the larger leaves with pieces of foam rubber where necessary.

Secure a small ball of green paste to the base of the flower. This will later be covered by the calyx.

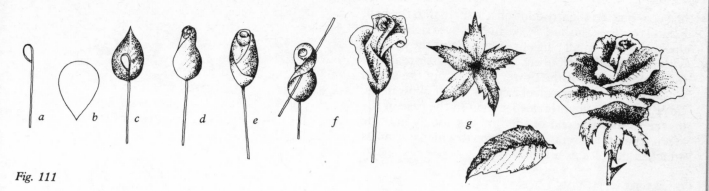

Fig. 111

Calyx: Use two pieces of modelling paste, one dark green, the other light green. Look at the calyx of a real flower and try to obtain the same colour by mixing the colours. Put the two pieces of paste on top of each other and roll them out until quite thin. Cut out the leaves, using a calyx cutter. Cut fine shreds in the leaves with a pair of nail scissors (Fig. 111g). Sprinkle a little cornflour on to the palm of your hand and put the "star" into your hand, light side facing down (the cornflour will give a pollen effect). Pull a small ball tool (the round end of a hatpin would also do) from the point of the leaf to its centre to make it curl. With the leaves still in the palm of your hand, make a hollow in the centre and pierce a hole in it. Turn the rose upside down, moisten the little green ball with egg white or water and insert the stem of the rose through the hole in the calyx. The calyx will now curl over with the light green on the inside. The curled leaves will thus be lighter green on top and darker green underneath. Carefully press around the ball. Let one or more sepals stand up slightly against the rose. Bend the stem of the rose and insert it into a piece of polystyrene, leaving the rose upside down to dry. You can bend the stem back later. The rose leaves are made in the same way as those for the dog rose.

3. Peach and apple blossoms

Stamens and petals: Make the stamens by wrapping the thread around one finger six times (Fig. 112a). Proceed by following the first method for the dog rose; the stamens remain on the thin fuse wire instead of being secured to florist's wire. Paint the ends of the stamens with pink vegetable colouring. Roll out pale pink and white modelling paste quite thinly. Cut out the flower by using a blossom cutter with a 20 mm diameter (Fig. 112b). Cut, roll and flute the petals according to the second method for the dog rose (Fig. 110f).

Place the flower on a piece of foam rubber and make a hollow in the middle with a small ball tool. Make a hole in the hollow through which to insert the wire with the stamens. Leave to dry.

Calyx: The calyx of the blossom is bell-shaped. Roll a small piece of green modelling paste into a cone. Flatten the fat end of the cone and roll out thin with a toothpick. Cut out the calyx by putting the calyx cutter over the cone (Fig. 112c). Roll each sepal until thin, make a hollow and pierce a hole in the middle.

Coat the leaves with egg white or water and attach to the flower. Insert the wire with the stamens into the flower and draw them through the calyx (Fig. 112d) until the stamens are neatly positioned in the centre of the flower. Pipe a dot of green royal icing in the centre of the stamens.

If the flower is white, only the backs of the leaves are lightly painted with pink powder colouring. If it is pink, paint the base on the inside of the flower a darker shade of pink.

BLOSSOM BUDS
Roll a small piece of modelling paste into a ball the size

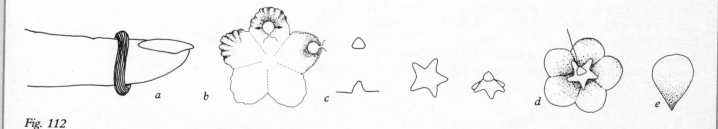

Fig. 112

of a pea. Flatten slightly and roll a stamen into the ball. Round the tip of the bud. Make five grooves right across the bud with a small pair of scissors. Paint the grooves with pink powder colouring. Make a tiny green calyx in the same way as for the flower, but cut out the sepals with a small knife instead of a cutter. The hollow in the calyx should be slightly deeper than in the case of the flower so that the end of the bud fits snugly and the green sepals fold over it. The stamen to which the bud is attached doubles as a stem.

BLOSSOM WITH FIVE LOOSE PETALS

Thinly roll out pink or white paste. Cut out five petals with a rose petal cutter, each with a 10 mm diameter (Fig. 112e). Cover with a piece of thin plastic. Put each petal into the palm of your hand, roll the edges until thin with a small ball tool and make a slight hollow in the centre. Place in a small hollow container, for example foam rubber with hollows (a bath mat will do). Finish all the petals and allow to dry slightly.

The instructions for the calyx and its finish are the same as for the flower, except that there are five loose petals that each has to be placed on a green sepal before the stamens are inserted and drawn through.

4. Forget-me-nots and other filler flowers

Use small bits of modelling paste at a time when making forget-me-nots. Roll out a piece of blue or pink modelling paste very thin and cut out a few flowers with a small blossom cutter (Fig. 113a). Use cutters in different sizes to make other filler flowers.

Put the flowers on a piece of foam rubber and roll a small ball tool over the leaves until they are very thin (Fig. 113b). Put the instrument in the centre of the flower and press gently to make a hollow. Insert a hole for the stamens and put the flowers into a board with hollows or a piece of foam rubber – a bath mat will do (see Fig. 113c). Leave to dry. Pipe a dot of yellow royal icing in the centre of each flower with a No 1 writing tube and attach the stamen to it (Fig. 113d). Let it dry.

SMALL FLOWER BUDS

Roll a tiny piece of modelling paste into a ball, insert the head of a stamen into it and flatten. Roll between your fingers to form a bud. The stamens for the bud and flowers serve as stems. You should therefore use top quality stamens. Alternatively, make your own.

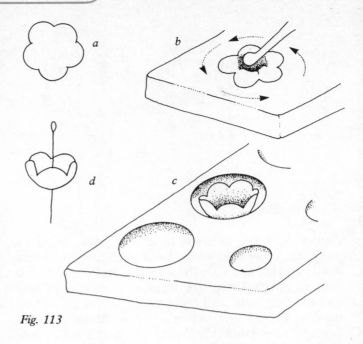

Fig. 113

5. Daisies

Petals: Cut a few plastic bags into thin strips and put them in a container. Roll out white or yellow modelling paste thinly. Use a daisy cutter to cut out the flowers (Fig. 114a). Place one flower on a piece of waxed paper on a flower nail. Cover the others with a piece of thin plastic. Divide each petal into two using a sharp knife and separate the petals slightly to form a circle. Flatten each leaf with a toothpick. Carefully remove the flower from the flower nail with a spatula and place on a piece of foam rubber. Make a slight hollow in the centre and make a hole. Gently "toss" the flower into the container with plastic strips. In this way it will dry naturally without looking stiff.

Fig. 114a

Calyx: Roll a piece of green paste the size of a pea into a cone. Flatten the sides at the wide end of the cone and shape with a toothpick to form a calyx. Press the calyx cutter over the calyx and roll each sepal to make it even thinner (Fig. 114b1).

Insert covered florist's wire (No 26) with a round, flat eye through the hole in the flower (Fig. 114b2). Coat the calyx with a little egg white or water, insert the wire through it and press against the flower.

Pipe yellow royal icing into the centre of the flower and sprinkle with yellow *nonpareils* (Fig. 114b3). Leave to dry. Paint the inside base of the petals with a little pale green powder colouring. Make the daisies in different sizes.

Fig. 114b

6. Stamens

Note: These stamens are *not* meant for flowers with very delicate stamens, for example dog roses. For them only very fine stamens should be used (see p. 76).

Ingredients
10 ml cold water
10 ml gelatine
10 ml warm water
cotton thread (not too thick) or thin crochet thread

Method
Pour the cold water into a bowl and sprinkle the gelatine over it. Place over a saucepan on low heat and add the hot water. Stir constantly until the gelatine has dissolved. Dip lengths of thread into the solution and strip off the gelatine between your fingers. Attach to the edge of the working surface so that it hangs straight. Leave to dry. Cut the thread in 50 mm lengths.

7. Arranging flowers and small corsages

Use covered florist's wire (No 26 or 28) and arrange the flowers, buds, single green leaves and florist's ribbon that has been cut in thin strips, to form sprays or posies (Fig. 115a and b).

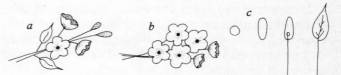

Fig. 115

Make a few small green leaves without using a cutter. Roll a small ball of paste into a sausage and insert the stamen into it. Press against a fresh leaf to get an impression of the veins and pinch the end to make it sharp (Fig. 115c). Curve slightly to give it a natural appearance.

8. Ivy leaves

These leaves (Fig. 116) are handy for any decoration. Match the colours with the natural colour of the leaves. Variations can be made by using cream-coloured modelling paste, putting avocado green powder colouring on the leaf and painting it with peppermint green powder colouring. The green colourings should be painted on unevenly. The cream-coloured paste should still be visible at the edge of the leaves. To give these or any other shiny leaf a naturally shiny appearance, pass them through the steam of a boiling kettle.

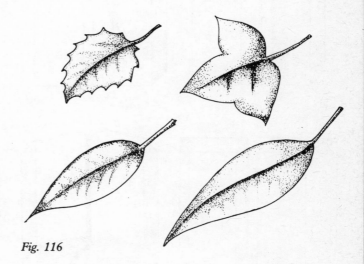

Fig. 116

CHAPTER 13

Miscellaneous

It is impossible to cover the entire spectrum of cake decoration and all the various techniques in one book. There are, however, a couple of things we would like to include here such as useful hints and decorations used on some of the cakes. We have not discussed all the cakes in detail because the photographs are quite clear and they are complemented by full-sized patterns.

1. A book made from a square cake
(Fig. 117)

Use either a book-shaped or a square cake tin. Bake a fruitcake which is neither too high nor too flat. Mark the centre line and a line 12 mm on either side (a). Using a sharp knife, cut diagonally through the cake from point X to point Y (b). You now have two pieces of cake, each with a long straight and a long slanted side. Turn piece 1 over so that the bottom side faces up and put the two straight sides together (c). Join them with a little melted apricot jam. Cut an indentation at the centre line or cut the top section of the cake to take on the shape of a book

(d). The cake can also be covered with marzipan in such a way that it looks like a book. The slanted sides of the cake form the outer sides of the book. The figures on the Christmas cake (Photograph 33 on p. 113) and the star (Fig. 118) are made directly on the cake with icing used for floodwork.

Fig. 118

2. Heart-shaped cake (made from a round and a square cake)

If you want to bake a 240 mm wide heart-shaped cake as indicated on Fig. 119, but do not have a heart-shaped tin, bake two cakes: one in a square tin with sides measuring 160 mm and one in a round tin with a 160 mm diameter. Ensure that the cakes are both the same height by measuring the depth of the cake mixture in the tins with a skewer before baking the cakes as usual.

To make the heart shape position the square cake in the shape of a diamond on a cake board. (If using a heart-shaped board the lower point of the diamond should correspond with the point of the heart.) Cut the round cake in half and attach the two halves with melted apricot jam to the upper sides of the diamond to complete the heart (Fig. 119).

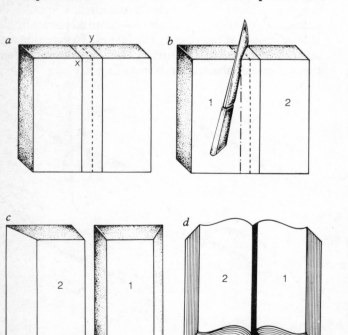

Fig. 117

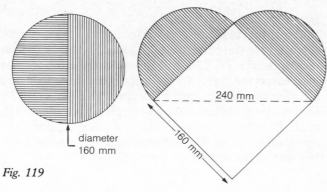

diameter
160 mm

240 mm

160 mm

Fig. 119

3. Lettering

Because the lettering on a cake is most important, you should practise until you become adept at handling the writing tube. Use royal icing which is not too stiff but not too runny either. Practise writing the examples at the back of the book by putting a piece of glass or tightly drawn plastic sheeting over the design. Perfect control of the icing bag is important especially where the letters curve and the pressure has to be increased slightly. Do not write directly on to the cake – hold the writing tube slightly above the surface of the cake and let the icing fall in the required position. Slanting letters should all be slanted at the same angle – work in the direction indicated by the arrows. We have also supplied examples of letters that you can flood beforehand and position on the cake at a later stage. (See examples on pp. 155 and 156.)

4. Mixture for shiny figures and leaves

Marzipan figures, flowers, fruit and leaves acquire a beautiful shine if coated with this mixture:

Ingredients
37,5 ml cold water
12,5 ml gum arabic (or gum acacia)

Method
Pour the water into a bowl and add the gum arabic. Put the bowl over boiling water and stir until all the gum has dissolved and the lumps have disappeared. Sieve through a piece of fine material, place in an airtight container and keep in the fridge. Using a small brush, coat the object with a thin layer of gum. Leave to dry. It might be necessary to coat the object with two to three layers to acquire the required shine.

This mixture is also useful for attaching petals to one another. When the gum arabic mixture is painted over a surface that has already been painted, however, some of the colouring might dissolve. If you want to colour the gum, add some paste or powder colouring.

5. Sugar rocks

Ingredients
cardboard box, 300 mm x 300 mm x 300 mm
waxed paper, greased
100 g icing sugar
half an egg white
dark brown and green colouring
1 kg sugar
250 ml warm water

Method
Line the cardboard box with the greased waxed paper. Mix the icing sugar and egg white as you would for royal icing – the mixture should be neither too stiff nor too runny. Colour the icing dark brown or green, depending on its intended use, for example, brown for rocks and green for bushes. Put the sugar and water into a saucepan and stir until the sugar has dissolved. Continually remove any crystals that form on the sides of the saucepan with a wet brush. Heat to 120 °C at sea-level. (Adjust the temperature in higher-lying areas.) Remove the syrup from the heat and stir in the royal icing. Stir quickly as the mixture might bubble over. Immediately pour into the cardboard box. Leave to cool. Break into pieces to form rocks and keep in an airtight container. To make sand, roll the pieces with a rolling-pin until fine.

6. Wet rocks and water

To make wet rocks for a pond, for example, mix a little gum arabic with warm water. When the gum has dissolved, add brown coloured paste or powder and paint the rocks with the mixture.

To make water for a dam, add sufficient water to sifted icing sugar to make a runny mixture. Colour it blue.

7. Background for children's cakes

Grass
Colour diluted royal icing pale green. Using a wide brush, cover the entire cake board with the icing on the areas where you want grass. Add a little dark green colouring to some of the icing and stir to make a stripy mixture (do not mix it well). Paint on the light green surface while still stripy.

Ground or sand
Dilute royal icing and colour it brown. Paint the ground or sandy areas with the mixture using a wide brush and sprinkle with finely ground sugar rocks.

8. Ornaments for christening cakes

(All the full-sized patterns appear at the back of this book.)

Umbrella and pillow (Fig. 120)

Roll out a thin piece of modelling paste and cut it out according to the pattern (Fig. 120a). The full-sized pattern appears on p.138. Flute all around the edge approximately 5 cm deep using a toothpick and carefully place it over a ball with a 400 mm diameter. Press down evenly, taking care not to flatten the fluted edge. (Secure the ball with Prestik Plasticine adhesive to prevent it rolling around.) Pierce a hole in the centre of the umbrella and leave to dry. Cover florist's wire (No 22) with white florist's ribbon and push 6 mm of the wire through the hole. Another few layers of adhesive tape around the wire will prevent the ribbon from coming loose. Pipe a dot of royal icing on the inside to prevent the wire from slipping through the hole. Bend the bottom of the handle and tie a ribbon around it. Embroider the outside of the umbrella (Fig. 120b).

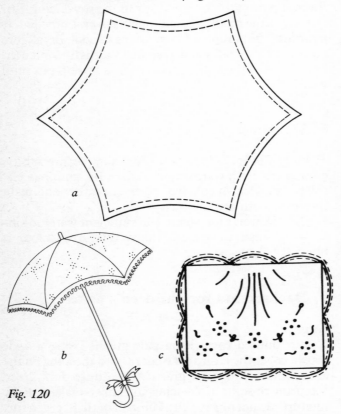

Fig. 120

Make a fondant pillow, crimp the edge and embroider it (Fig. 120c). Make an indent for the doll's head. If you do not have a suitable mould for the doll, use a real doll. Use thinly rolled-out paste to make the blanket and drape it over the doll. Decorate according to taste. (Also see Photograph 36 on p. 116.)

Bib (Fig. 121)

Roll out the modelling paste thinly and cut out a bib according to the pattern (Fig. 121a). The full-sized pattern appears on p. 139. Lift the edge of the bib at intervals. Insert the cone (X), made from the thin inner lid of a coffee tin, underneath to support the bib until dry. Embroider the bib and attach two pieces of ribbon to the neck. Put the bib on the cake and place a small floral spray underneath the section where the cone lifted the bib. (See Photograph 48 on p. 128.)

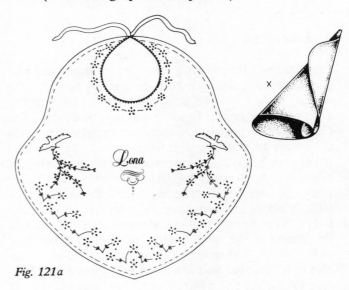

Fig. 121a

Baby bootees (large – Fig. 121 b-f, small – Fig. 122)

Roll out modelling paste until it is 2,5 mm thick and cut out two soles according to the pattern (Fig. 121). The full-sized patterns appear on p. 139. Roll out the paste thinly and cut two uppers for the bootees (Fig. 121c). Paint a little gum arabic approximately 2 mm from one edge of the upper (the seam), fold over and press (Fig. 121d). Paint gum arabic along the edge of the sole, place the upper on top and press along the sides with a small flat instrument. If the cake is for a baby girl, cut an ankle strap and make a button and buttonhole (Fig. 121e). Pierce two holes in the bootee and thread with a ribbon if the cake is for a baby boy (Fig. 121f). Make a left and a right bootee. (See Photograph 48 on p. 128.)

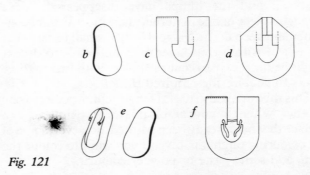

Fig. 121

Dress and small matching bootees (Fig. 122a)
Roll out modelling paste thinly and cut out the pattern for the skirt (1 in Fig. 122a). Cut out the armholes. Scallop the hem and fold in the pleats. Using the same pattern, make a petticoat that is slightly narrower. Coat with a little gum arabic and put the dress on top of it. Flatten the pleats at the top and fold in the sides by 3 mm to give the dress a well-finished appearance. Lift the pleats slightly and insert the cone (X), made from the thin inner lid of a coffee tin, underneath one of the pleats. The floral spray will later be inserted at this spot.

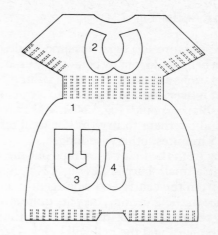

Fig. 122b

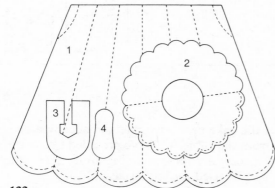

Fig. 122a

Roll out another piece of modelling paste thinly and cut out the bodice according to the pattern (2 in Fig. 122a) or cut it out with a scalloped biscuit cutter. Scallop the bottom edge of the front, fold it in half and paint with a little gum on the inside. Insert the skirt between the two pieces. Press, but be careful not to flatten the scalloped edge. Embroider the dress. Cut out bootees (3 and 4 in Fig. 122a). The soles should be 2 mm thick – assemble them as shown (Fig. 121). Make a card with the baby's name written on it (Fig. 123a). (See Photograph 48 on p. 128.)

Note: The design of these bootees matches the dress. (The full-sized pattern is on p. 140.)

Crawler and matching bootees (Fig. 122b)
Roll out the modelling paste thinly and cut out the crawler and collar according to the pattern (1 and 2 in Fig. 122b). The full-sized pattern appears on p. 140. Crimp the marked sections with a crimper to pleat them slightly. Position the collar and fold back slightly. Fold in the sides by 3 mm to give a neat appearance. Before drying the sleeves and trouser sections, insert pieces of cotton or foam rubber underneath them. Cut out the bootees (3 and 4 in Fig. 122b) and assemble them as shown (Fig. 121). The soles must be 2 mm thick. Make a card with the baby's name written on it and arrange some tiny flowers on the cake (Fig. 123b). (See Photograph 48 on p. 128.)

a

b

Fig. 123

9. Sugar bells (Fig. 124)

Using the mixture for sugar ornaments described on p. 14, fill a bell mould (or any bell – those used as Christmas decorations are ideal) (Fig. 124a). Tamp down well. Now turn it over and tap it gently to loosen the sugar. Carefully lift the mould (Fig. 124b). Make several sugar bells and allow them to dry (in hot weather approximately 15 minutes, otherwise longer).

Starting from the first bell, scrape out the soft sugar inside with a small sharp knife (Fig. 124c). Always start scraping from the centre and work gently towards the sides. Once the bells are dry, they are quite strong, but if you delay scraping out the inside too long, the sugar will become too hard and the bell will break. Decorate the bells with edible glitter (see p. 14) or paint the edges with a brush. When making coloured bells, colour the mixture beforehand.

When dry, make a clapper by laying a line inside with a No 2 tube and royal icing. Place a silver dragee at the end of the line, on the edge of the bell.

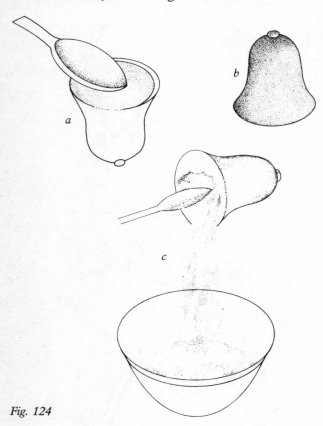

Fig. 124

10. Church window (Fig. 125)

The cake for a golden wedding anniversary on p. 127 is decorated with a church window (Fig. 125a). It can also be used for a Christmas cake (Fig. 125b) when placed

Fig. 125

flat on the cake or at an angle and accompanied by a verse from the Bible. We have provided two patterns – one is specifically for a wedding anniversary and the other can be used for any occasion.

Roll out a piece of modelling paste (see p. 19) between two layers of plastic sheeting until paper-thin. Remember, the window must be transparent. Put the pattern on the plastic sheeting and, with a sharp knife, cut out the frame through both layers of plastic sheeting. (The full-sized pattern appears on p. 141.) You may use a pair of scissors to cut the frame, but be careful not to stretch the paste.

Note: The layers of plastic sheeting should remain on the paste to prevent it stretching.

Place the window on a level surface and carefully remove the top plastic sheeting. Leave the paste to dry slightly. Place it on the pattern which should be visible through the plastic sheeting and paste if the paste has been rolled out thinly enough. Pipe the frame of the window and the design on the inside using royal icing and a No 0 or No 00 tube. (The frame may be piped with a No 1 tube, but the inside design requires a very fine tube.) Flood the frame (including the figures and rings in the case of the anniversary cake) with soft icing. Leave for a day or two to dry. Turn over and remove the bottom layer of plastic sheeting. Leave to dry properly on both sides. If the window is to be placed on the cake in an upright position, flood the frame at the back as well. If the window is to be used flat on the cake, place the pattern on an even surface, cover with a piece of plastic sheeting and secure with drawing pins or adhesive tape. Flood the frame first. Leave to dry. Turn it over and carefully remove the plastic. Put a clean layer of plastic sheeting over the pattern. Reposition the frame on the design. Complete the fine decoration on the inside of the frame, taking care not to move the frame. Dry thoroughly. Turn over and carefully peel off the plastic sheeting. Lift the window slightly at the top so that it lies at an angle.

11. Plaques (Fig. 126)

Here are a few examples of plaques that can be used on cakes or as name-cards at parties. If large enough, they can serve as the only decoration on a cake. Plaques are very popular and sell well at cake sales. People who cannot decorate cakes buy them to use as the only decoration on a cake. Plaques are usually made from *pastillage* but modelling paste can also be used (see Chapter 2 for recipes).

Note: Plaques must be turned over frequently while drying to prevent them warping. They should be neatly finished with dots or a line. If lettering is to be done, first ensure that the plaque or scroll is thoroughly dry.

Plaque a is made of two identical pieces of *pastillage*. One is cut in the centre as indicated by X on the illustration. Fold or roll the corners of the triangles outward (see Photograph 48 on p. 128). When both pieces have dried thoroughly they are glued together with a mixture of gum acacia and water. The opening can be filled with flowers.

Fig. 126 a

Plaque b also consists of two identical pieces of *pastillage*. An oval or circle is cut out of one and two corresponding holes are pierced through both. When they have dried thoroughly the two pieces are bound together like a book with a ribbon. The bottom piece can be decorated with flowers or writing.

Plaque c is a name-card. A wedge is fixed to the back

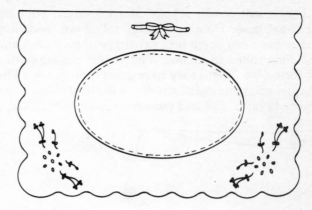

Fig. 126 b

to make it stand. Both pieces should be completely dry before they are glued together.

Plaque d can be used on top of a cake as a name-card, or the outer edge can be made separately and, when it

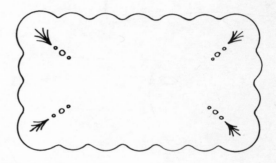

Fig. 126 c

has dried, glued to the bottom piece. The bottom piece can be decorated with lettering (see Photograph 39 on p. 119) or flowers.

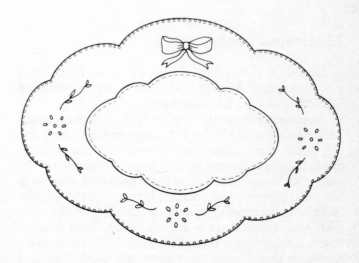

Fig. 126 d

Parchment scrolls (e) are also extremely popular. They are made from very thinly rolled-out modelling paste. They can be cut into any shape or even torn, and the ends rolled in or out. The scrolls are supported by cotton wool until they have dried thoroughly. (The plaques and parchment scrolls are illustrated in Photograph 48 on p. 128 and patterns appear on p. 142.)

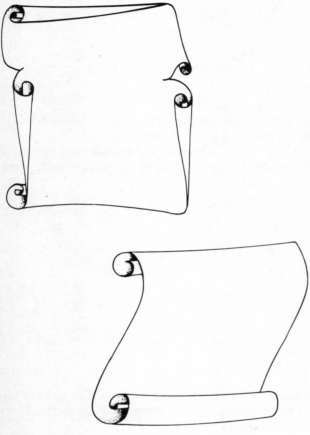

Fig. 126 e

12. Draped cloth

A draped cloth was used on one of the wedding cakes (see Photograph 44 on p. 124). On its own it serves as an attractive and useful decoration.

To make it, roll out the fondant which has been mixed and kneaded with a little CMC, or gum tragacanth and egg white, until it measures 1 mm. Cut out a circle, approximately 50 mm bigger than the top surface of the cake. Pick it up carefully and place over the cake which has been covered with fondant beforehand. Drape the cloth by making small horizontal folds in it. Paint these folds with gum acacia or egg white and keep them in position by securing them to the cake with toothpicks. Leave to dry. Carefully remove the toothpicks and cover the holes with bows or flowers.

13. Cut-up cakes

Toddlers have very powerful imaginations and it is not necessary to make their cakes absolutely realistic. They are, furthermore, more interested in eating the cake than in its appearance!

Accordingly it is unnecessary to go to a great deal of trouble to decorate a cake for a toddler. Rather decorate it with plenty of sweets, biscuits, etc.

Cakes which can be cut according to a pattern are recommended. It is also a good idea to leave the cake in the fridge for about half an hour before cutting it to prevent it crumbling unnecessarily. A sponge cake (recipe on p. 11) and seven-minute frosting (recipe on p. 16) can be recommended. The tiger (Fig. 127 and 128) is a good example of a cut-up cake.

Study Photograph 20 on p. 100 and follow the instructions (1, 2 and 3) on the illustration to fit the different sections together. (Full-sized patterns appear on pp. 143 and 144.)

Fig. 127

Fig. 128

Requirements
a round sponge cake with a 200 mm diameter
a square sponge cake with 230 mm sides
seven-minute frosting
modelling paste

Method
Use the patterns on pp. 143 and 144 (Fig. 127 and 128) and cut out the cake in sections 1, 2 and 3 as indicated. Arrange on a large cake board in the shape of a tiger. Cover the cake with the seven-minute frosting and use modelling paste for the eyes, nose and mouth. Use light brown colouring or cocoa to make the stripes.

14. Dwarf cake (Photograph 21 on p. 101)

The description for modelled dwarfs appears on p. 71.

The stem of the toadstool is the actual cake. Use half of the ingredients for a dark fruitcake (see p. 12). Pour the mixture into an ovenproof dish or tin with a 150 mm diameter and bake for 1 hour at 120 °C and then at 110 °C for 2 hours.

The top section of the toadstool cannot be made from cake as it will be too heavy for the stem. Make it as follows, using polystyrene. Glue together with a suitable adhesive two circles with 160 mm and 220 mm diameters respectively. Each must be 70 mm deep. Sand the two pieces into the required shape with medium sandpaper. Make it slightly hollow where the stem has to fit into the cap. Study the cake in Photograph 21, p. 101. Cover the stem with marzipan and pale green plastic icing and put it on a thick cake board with a 400 mm diameter.

Roll out a piece of brown modelling paste and make an impression of a real vine leaf on it. Remove the leaf and carefully cut out the pattern along the edge. This is the door. Glue it to the cake with gum arabic and tidy it up. The windows are made from coloured paste and are glued to the stem. Thinly roll out a small piece of brown gum paste, cut it into strips and glue to the windows to form the frames. Make a flower box filled with forget-me-nots below the window.

To cover the cap, coat the entire surface with a thin layer of royal icing. Roll out a small piece of white fondant until it is 6 mm thick and secure it to the underside of the cap. Using a knife, cut grooves about 60 mm in length right around the underside of the cap. First paint them light brown and then apply some dark brown powder colouring here and there.

Paint the top with diluted royal icing. Roll out a piece of red fondant for the top. Rub until smooth and neatly finish the edge by folding it in slightly over the grooved underside. Thinly roll out some white fondant, cut out circles and glue them to the top of the cap. Complete the decoration with sugar rocks (instructions on p. 83) and flowers. Sweets and coloured popcorn can also be used as flowers.

15. Ladybird cake (Photograph 22 on p. 102)

Use the cherry and sultana cake on p. 12. The cake usually comes out round at the top and is therefore ideal for a rounded ladybird cake.

Put 375 g of the mixture into a small, round ovenproof dish with a 130 mm diameter. Put the rest of the mixture into a round tin with diameter 200 mm and height 75 mm. Bake for 50-60 minutes at 180 °C.

Cut a piece off each cake so that they fit neatly against each other. Put the large cake on a cake board 400 mm in diameter. Cut the underside of the head level so that it lies flat on the board. Secure the head to the body with melted apricot jam. Cover with marzipan and fondant. First use white fondant and then a thin layer of red fondant – too much red colouring will give the fondant a bitter taste, therefore use it sparingly unless you have tasteless red colouring.

Thinly roll out a small piece of black fondant, cut out nine circles and secure to the body with gum acacia or egg white. Cut a groove right across the body. Separate the head and the body with a black strip and glue an oval piece of black fondant to the front of the head. Use white and black fondant for the eyes. Roll a piece of black fondant into a thin sausage and put on the board around the bottom of the cake. Roll out another sausage, shape the legs and attach them to the body.

16. Car (Photograph 23 on p. 103)

Bake a 330 mm x 110 mm x 100 mm fruitcake. Cut out the shape of the car as well as the hollows for the wheels. Cover the cake (including the bottom) with marzipan and fondant. Use a crimper to achieve the different effects.

Use four ginger biscuits with strips of black fondant or liquorice around the edges for the wheels. Spikes and hub caps can be piped on to the biscuits and then painted silver. Make lights, numberplates and windscreen wipers.

Put the cake on a small 270 mm x 90 mm x 20 mm cake board and put this board on a larger one. (The cake should be slightly lifted with polystyrene, or it will look as if the car had got stuck in the mud!) Attach the wheels with royal icing. Pipe a row of shells around the bottom of the cake (see p. 40).

17. Train (Photograph 24 on p. 104)

Bake two sponge cakes, measuring 300 mm x 100 mm x 50 mm and 240 mm x 100 mm x 40 mm respectively, and bake two small round cakes in 410 g tins filled halfway with batter. A Swiss roll can also be used instead of the small cakes.

To make the train, cut the cakes according to the instructions in Fig. 129. Decorate the engine and then the coaches with butter icing. Finish each coach with a shell border before positioning the next one. Finish the cake with shells (see p. 40). Attach the wheels and fill the coaches with sweets.

The coaches can be made from gingerbread as a variation. Roll out the gingerbread dough thinly, press flat on a biscuit tray and bake. Cool and cut out the pieces for each of the coaches – a floor and four sides to match the engine. Attach with royal icing. Leave to dry and fill the coaches with sweets or coloured popcorn.

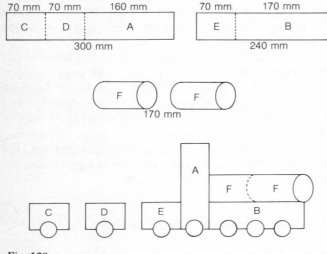

Fig. 129

18. Clown (Photograph 25 on p. 105)

Bake two round fruitcakes, 230 mm and 130 mm in diameter respectively. Use the smaller cake for the face and cover with flesh-coloured fondant.

Cover the large cake with white fondant. Colour three pieces of fondant in different colours, roll out until 1 mm thick and cut out circles 230 mm, 225 mm and 220 mm in diameter. Flute the edges by lifting them at intervals with ice-cream cones. Leave to dry thoroughly and position on the white cake. Attach to the cake and to each other with royal icing.

Roll a round nose in red modelling paste and attach with a piece of spaghetti and royal icing. Paint the face, place on the cake and attach with royal icing. Insert a piece of macaroni through the head and body, pipe hair with brown butter icing and a No 5 star tube and put a decorated ice-cream cone on the head. Cut out coloured circles and attach to the cake. Pipe a row of shells around the bottom of the cake (see p. 40).

19. Bunnies for twins (Photograph 26a on p.106)

Bake two light fruitcakes or cherry and sultana cakes in round ovenproof bowls with diameter 150 mm, and two small cakes in bowls with diameter 100 mm. Cover the cakes with marzipan. Shape the back legs with white gum paste and scratch the legs with a fork to give them a furry appearance.

Measure the two large cakes and cut out coloured fondant circles. Flute the edges as for the Garrett frill (see p. 42) and place over the bodies. Take care not to stretch the circles. Shape the front legs, scratch with a fork and attach to the top of the bodies with royal icing. Cut out a small circle, flute the edge and place on top of the front legs.

Use the two smaller cakes for the faces. Cover with fondant, scratch with a fork and cut grooves in which to insert the ears. Pipe a little soft icing on top of the body, position the head on top and insert a piece of macaroni through the head and into the body to keep it in position. Cover the holes. Paint the faces. Cut out four cardboard or rice paper bunny ears, insert into the head and attach with royal icing. Shape carrots and put the candles into them.

Easter eggs (Photograph 26b on p. 106) can be made according to the illustrations in Fig. 135 on pp. 151 and 152. Use white moulded sugar eggs and fondant to make the figures.

20. Strawberry cake (Photograph 27a on p. 107)

Bake the cake in two ovenproof pudding bowls – one slightly larger than the other. Place the bigger cake on top of the smaller cake. Cover with marzipan and fondant (see pp. 15 and 18). Make small notches at an angle in the surface of the cake to give it the appearance of a strawberry.

Use modelling paste to make the doll. Press the paste into a doll mould or use a real doll. Use different colours thinly rolled-out modelling paste for the clothes.

The same method can be used for making the apple cake in Photograph 27b on p. 107, this time using two ovenproof mixing bowls. Hollow out the top of the cake and cover it with marzipan. Follow the instructions on p.73 for making the worms.

21. Doll (Photograph 28 on p. 108)

Bake the cake in an ovenproof mixing bowl or a similar container. Use a long-legged doll. Remove the legs (they can be replaced at a later stage). Cut out a small 25 mm x 25 mm square and insert the doll's body into the hole. Cover the cake with marzipan. Correct the height of the cake with marzipan if necessary.

To make the doll's dress (Fig. 130 and full-sized pattern on p. 145), cut out a fondant panel from the waist to the hem (a). Do not roll out too thin. Moisten the marzipan and press the fondant panel to the front of the

skirt. Decorate it with any design you like. Use the Garrett frill technique to make the frills. The first frill is secured on both sides of the panel with egg white. Another three rows of frills are attached right round the skirt. Mark the scalloped pattern on the back of the skirt (b) so that you know where the frills should end. Continue attaching more frills right up to these marks. The frills will become shorter and shorter as you go along.

Thinly roll out a piece of pink modelling paste and cut out the pattern (b). Moisten the marzipan and attach the scalloped panel to it. Lift it slightly at the marks (x) and keep in position with toothpicks. Remove the toothpicks when dry. Pipe a little royal icing into the holes and put a flower on top. If preferred, the entire skirt can be covered in frills.

To make the bodice, roll out some paste and cut out the front (c) and the back (d). Carefully attach to the body. Cover the joins and the entire body with dots. Pipe dots around the neck for the string of pearls and cut out a large paste bow for the back of the dress. To make the hat, thinly roll out a piece of paste and cut out a circle with a biscuit cutter. Lay it over a rolling-pin or glass to dry in a rounded shape. Attach it to the doll's head with royal icing and make the crown of the hat with flowers.

A soft cake can also be used for the doll cake, The decoration can be done right round, by means of the frill tube (see p. 41). Cover the bodice with stars.

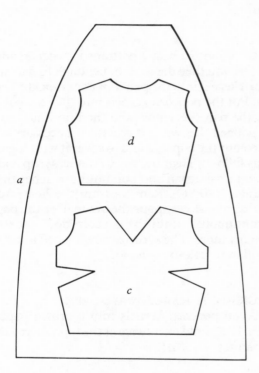

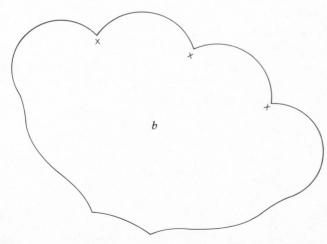

Fig. 130

22. Rondavel cake (Photograph 29 on p. 109)

Bake two round 180 mm x 180 mm cherry and sultana cakes or light fruitcakes. Cut them level and place one on top of the other, with a layer of melted apricot jam between them. Cover with marzipan and fondant and put on a round cake board with a 400 mm diameter.

Mark the bricks as illustrated in the photograph (p. 109) and lightly paint with powder colouring. Make a door and window with a curtain from modelling paste and place in position.

To give the cake extra height, place it on a piece of diagonally cut polystyrene before placing it on the cake board. Cover the slanted sides with brown royal icing and sprinkle them with sand (see p. 83).

Cover the cake board with green royal icing and sprinkle with green coconut. Decorate with rocks and flowers as illustrated in the photograph. Make the roof from a round piece of cardboard. Draw a circle with a 300 mm diameter and cut out a quarter. Staple the ends together and secure with adhesive tape. Cover with strips of overlapping red fondant or with royal icing and sprinkle with chocolate vermicelli. Place on top of the rondavel and finish with a row of small shells around the edge.

23. Snow White's seven dwarfs (Photograph 30 on p. 110)

The bed is made from an oblong light fruitcake covered with marzipan and fondant. The head and foot of the bed are made from *pastillage*. The dwarfs' faces are made from modelling paste using a Father Christmas mould – but they all have slightly different expressions. The blanket is also made from modelling paste. See the photograph on p. 110 for more detail.

24. Man's cake (Photograph 40 on p. 120)

The cake is in the shape of a desk. The man's interests or hobby can be illustrated by making a plaque (see p. 87) and placing it upright on the desk. In this case he is a physicist.

Bake an oblong dark fruitcake and shape according to the photograph. Cover with marzipan. To achieve the wood grain effect, use light and dark fondant to make three light and three dark rolls. Arrange the rolls next to each other alternately and stretch and fold them three or four times until the grain shows clearly. Roll out and cover the cake. Mark the drawers and attach the handles. Draw the microscope (or anything symbolising the man's interests) on the plaque and cut out the books in *pastillage* according to the patterns on p. 154. Leave to dry. Complete according to the three-dimensional floodwork technique. Colour vermicelli by rolling it in colouring diluted with water. Leave to dry. Pipe tips on to the ends with royal icing and paint the tips black to make pencils. Make a blotting pad and a notebook from thinly rolled-out modelling paste. Crumple up a few pieces of "paper" (thinly roll-out paste with lettering on it) and arrange on the desk. Use light and dark coconut for the carpet.

25. Coloured popcorn

Popcorn in different colours doubles up as a decoration or as flowers on a child's cake. Children also enjoy eating it.

Ingredients
45 ml cooking oil
125 ml popcorn kernels
250 ml sugar
125 ml water
15 ml golden syrup
7 ml margarine
colouring

Method
Pour the oil into a heavy-bottomed saucepan and heat well. Test whether the oil is hot enough by putting one popcorn kernel into the pan. If it pops quickly, the oil is ready. Put the popcorn kernels into the pan, cover and shake the pan every now and then until all the corns have popped. Repeat the process if necessary.

To colour the popcorn and to cover it with sugar, proceed as follows: Heat the sugar, water, syrup and margarine in a saucepan and boil until it reaches the hard ball stage (120 °C). Remove from the heat. Add the colouring and slowly pour the syrup over the popcorn. Stir continuously until the popcorn does not stick together any more. The syrup can be divided into batches and different colouring added.

POPCORN IN THE MICROWAVE OVEN
Put 100 ml popcorn kernels into a brown paper bag 260 mm long. Fold over twice at the top. Microwave for two minutes at HIGH.

Weights and measures

Lengths

1 millimetre	(mm)	=	0,039 inch
1 centimetre	(cm)	=	0,39 inch
1 metre	(m)	=	39,37 inch

Fluid measures

5 ml	=	1 metric teaspoon
12,5 ml	=	1 metric tablespoon
250 ml	=	1 metric cup
	=	200 g sugar
	=	130 g icing sugar
	=	225 g butter
	=	120 g flour

Weights

1 gram (g)	=	0,035 ounces
200 gram (g)	=	7 ounces
250 gram (g)	=	½ pound
500 gram (g)	=	1 pound

Oven temperatures

Celsius		Fahrenheit
100°	=	200°
110°	=	225°
130°	=	250°
140°	=	275°
150°	=	300°
170°	=	325°
180°	=	350°
190°	=	375°
200°	=	400°
220°	=	425°
230°	=	450°
240°	=	475°

Terminology

SOUTH AFRICAN	AMERICAN
butter icing	buttercream
cake board	cake tray
castor sugar	granulated sugar
cocoa	cocoa powder
cotton wool	cotton
extension work	bridge work
fruit-cake	pound cake
golden syrup	corn syrup
greaseproof paper	parchment paper
Holsum (vegetable fat)	Crisco
icing	frosting
icing bag	frosting cone
icing sugar	powdered or confectioner's sugar
icing tube	tip or nozzle
liquid glucose	karo or light corn syrup
marzipan	almond paste
mealies	corn
spatula	palette knife

Notes

Photographs

17. *Examples of marbling and feathering as well as flowers piped directly on to cup-cakes (see p. 43). Note the use of piping gel and side finishes such as crumbs, roasted coconut and chocolate vermicelli.*

18. *Different piped finishes and piped flowers made directly on cakes and cup-cakes.*
19. *Examples of piped flowers made on a flower nail, as well as symmetrical and asymmetrical decorations. These decorations can also be done in butter or royal icing. Note how one basic pattern can look different every time through the use of different tubes or colours. The patterns are on pp. 157 and 158.*

20. *The technique for cakes made for cutting is described on p. 88 and the pattern for the tiger appears on pp. 143 and 144 (Fig. 127 and 128).*
21. *A dwarf cake that will delight any child. The toadstool is described in full on p. 89 and the modelling of the dwarf on p. 71.*

22. *The ladybird cake is a real treat for children. Detailed instructions on how to make it appear on p. 89.*

23. *The car is perfect for a little boy. Refer to p. 89 for detailed instructions.*

24. *Children find the magic of a train irresistible, and there are enough treats in the gingerbread coaches to satisfy one and all. Detailed instructions on how to make the train and popcorn are on pp. 90 and 92.*
25. *The clown is another firm favourite with children. Instructions for making this cake appear on p. 90.*

26a and b. *Twins often have to share one cake. These two bunnies will solve the problem. The Easter eggs are for their friends. For detailed instructions on how to make the bunnies, see p. 90. See Fig. 135 on pp. 151 and 152 for examples of Easter eggs.*

27a and b. *The strawberry cake is not only delicious but decorated with a doll as well. The whole apple cake is edible – even the worms! Detailed instructions on how to make these cakes are given on p. 90.*

28. *The doll used here will delight a little girl for many years to come. Detailed instructions on how to make her clothes and the doll itself appear on p. 91.*

29. *The rondavel cake with the witch and other figures are described in detail on p. 91.*

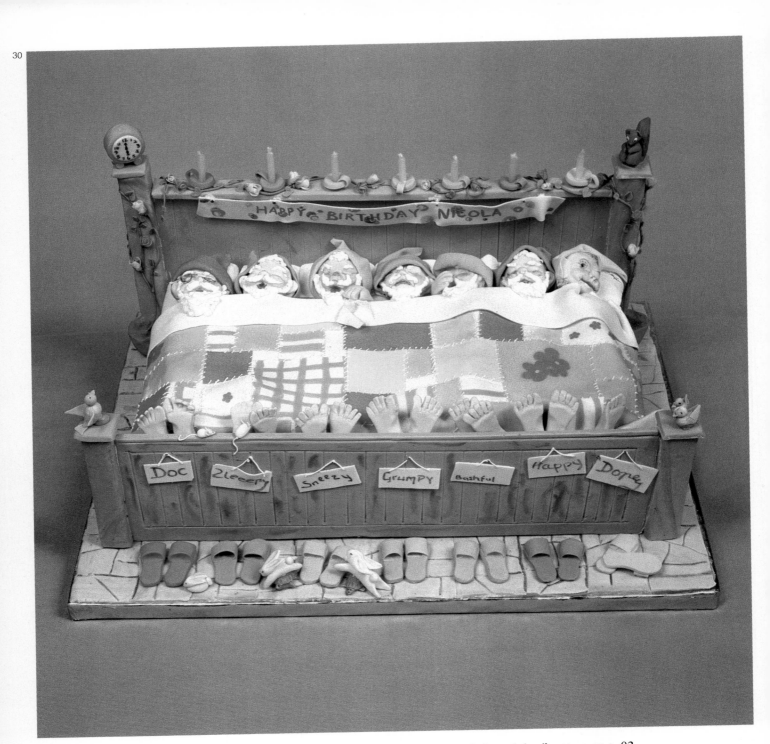

30. *Snow White's seven dwarfs are having a snooze. This cake was made by Mary Lake and details appear on p. 92.*

31. *The collar for this Christmas cake was made with icing used for floodwork (see Fig. 85a on p. 134). The poinsettia was modelled.*

32. *The bells on this cake are made of castor sugar (see p. 86, Fig. 124) and the cake has been finished with crimping and extension work. Details of these techniques appear on pp. 61 and 62.*

33. *The Nativity scene is always popular for Christmas cakes. On p. 82 we explain how to make a book without a special tin. The writing and figures (Fig. 118 on p. 137) were done with icing used for floodwork. Kate Venter made this magnificent cake.*

34. *A christening cake for a little boy. The little modelling paste boy was made in a bought mould. The scroll was made from thinly rolled out modelling paste (see Fig. 126 on p. 142). The Garrett frill is described on p. 42 (Fig. 54). This cake was made by Eulogia Murray.*

35. *The bib collar for this christening cake is made from icing used for floodwork (see the pattern on p. 146). The cake was made by Eulogia Murray.*

36. *This unusual christening cake is suitable for a baby boy or girl. The baby is made from modelling paste in a bought mould. Full instructions on how to make the umbrella are given on p. 84 and the pattern appears on p. 138 (Fig. 120).*

116

37. *This engagement cake was created by Kate Venter and the flowers were all made on a flower nail. Details of this technique and the steps for making the different flowers (Fig. 73 and 74) appear on p. 51.*

38. *A twenty-first birthday is an important day in anyone's life and Dora van Heerden has decorated this cake for a young man who is a keen rider. The horses on top of the cake were made with icing used for floodwork. Those on the side are good examples of cocoa painting described on p. 42. Patterns for the horses appear on p. 153 (Fig. 136a and b).*
39. *This birthday cake for a woman was made by Gwyn Müller. The flowers were modelled (see p. 79, Fig. 111). The name-card (see Fig. 126 on p. 142) is made of pastillage. The Garrett frill (Fig. 54) is discussed in detail on p. 42.*

38

118

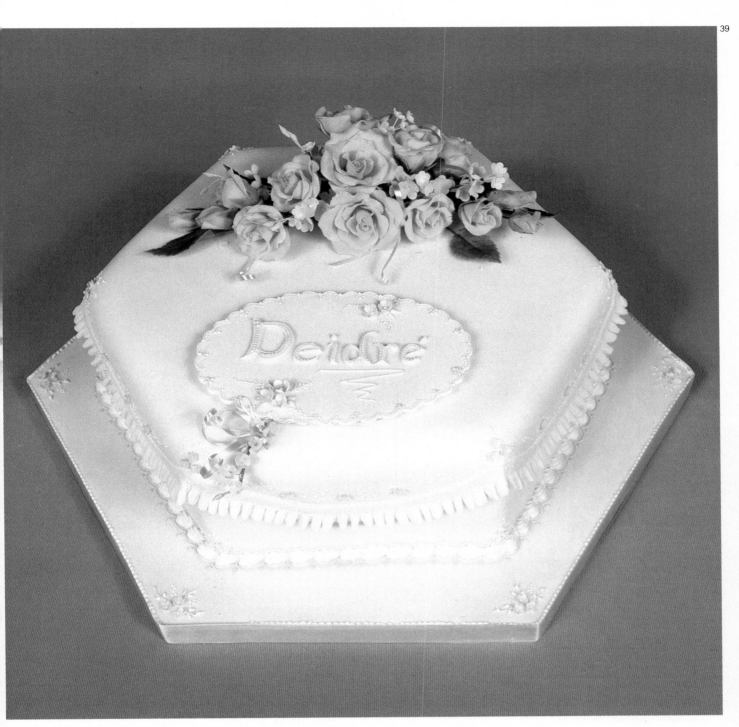

40. *A man's birthday poses quite a problem. Usually his hobby or profession is depicted. This cake was made for a physicist but can be adapted for any profession by simply changing the plaque. A full description of the cake appears on p. 92. The patterns can be found on p. 154 (Fig. 137).*

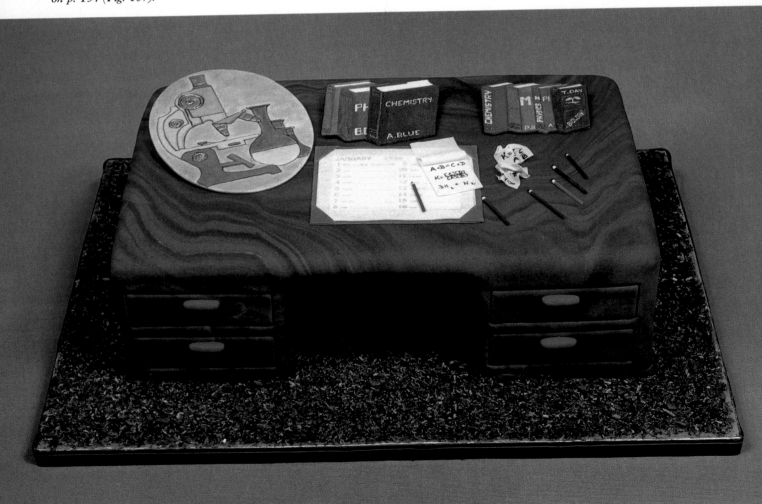

41. *Depicting somebody's hobby is always a success. This cake for a young gymnast was made by Eulogia Murray under the supervision of Kate Venter. The figures are made of icing used for floodwork and the patterns appear on p. 147 (Fig. 132).*

42. *The decorations for this Mother's Day cake beautifully illustrates the use of the Kinnie crimper. Details appear on pp. 67 and 68 (Fig. 99). This cake was made by Gwyn Müller.*

43. *This ballerina cake was made by Kate Venter. Both the collar and ballerina were made with icing used for floodwork and the patterns appear on pp. 129 and 148 (Fig. 81c and 133). The technique is described on p. 56.*

44. *The wedding cake with its draped cloth is described on p. 88 and the modelled flowers are described on p. 79 (Fig.111).*

45. *Cake decorators who think only modelled flowers will do for a wedding cake should take a closer look at this wedding cake with piped flowers, designed and decorated by Kate Venter. The steps for making the proteas are described in detail on p. 52 (Fig. 76).*

46. *This cake for a silver wedding anniversary might be a bit advanced for a beginner but if the instructions for fine filigree on p. 38 are followed carefully there should be no problem. The patterns for the filigree ornaments appear on p. 149 (Fig. 134a and b).*

47. *A cake for a golden wedding anniversary depicts the autumn of married life and the church window symbolises the secret of a happy marriage. The cake was designed and made by Eulogia Murray. The ribbon inserts and crimping are described on p. 65 (Fig. 96) and the church window is described on p. 86. The pattern (Fig. 125a) appears on p. 141.*

48. *Plaques and scrolls add interest to any cake. Instructions for making them appear on p. 87 and patterns (Fig. 126) on p. 142. For christening cakes, ornaments made of modelling paste (see pp. 84 and 85) can be placed on the plaques.*

Patterns

Fig. 80 *Patterns for floodwork as described on pp. 55-57.*

Fig. 81 a, b and c *Patterns for floodwork. Fig. 81c is used for the ballerina cake (Photograph 43 on p. 123).*

Fig. 81 d, e and f *Extra patterns for floodwork.*

Fig. 82 *Patterns for Christmas ornaments in icing used for floodwork as described on p. 57.*

Fig. 84a *Pattern for symmetrical collar as described on p. 58.*

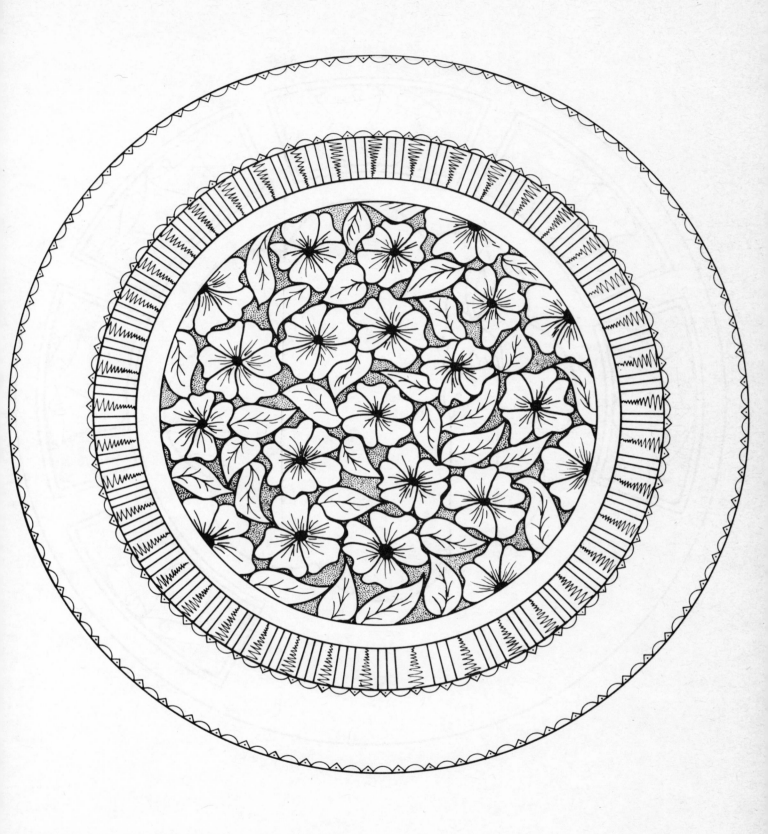

Fig. 84b *Pattern for symmetrical collar as described on p. 58.*

133

Fig. 85a *Pattern for Christmas cake collar (Photograph 31 on p. 111) as described on p. 58.*

Fig. 85b *Pattern for collar as described on p. 59.*

Fig. 86 . *Patterns for plaques done in three-dimensional floodwork (Photograph 48 on p. 128) as described on p. 59.*

Fig. 87 *Pattern for stork plaque on a christening cake (Photograph 48 on p. 128) as described on p. 60.*

Fig. 118 *Figures on the Christmas cake (Photograph 33 on p. 113).*

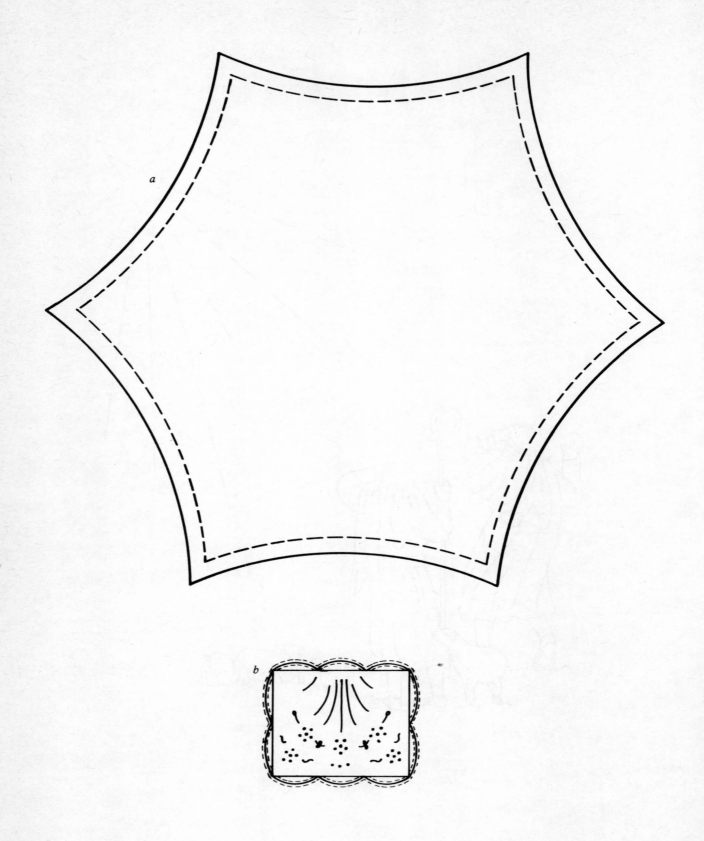

Fig. 120 *Patterns for umbrella and pillow for a christening cake (Photograph 36 on p. 116) as described on p. 84.*

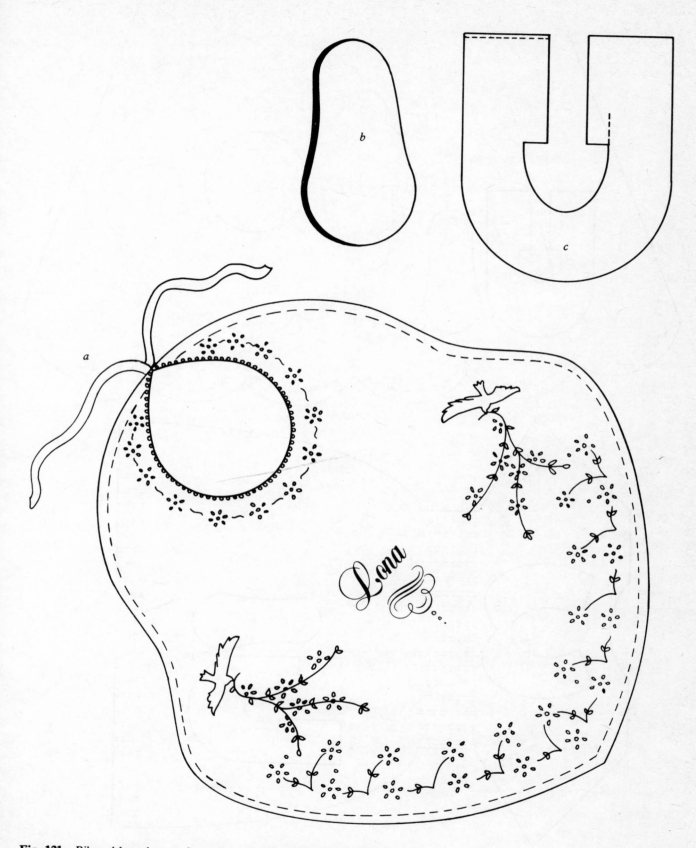

Fig. 121 *Bib and large bootees for a christening cake as described on p. 84.*

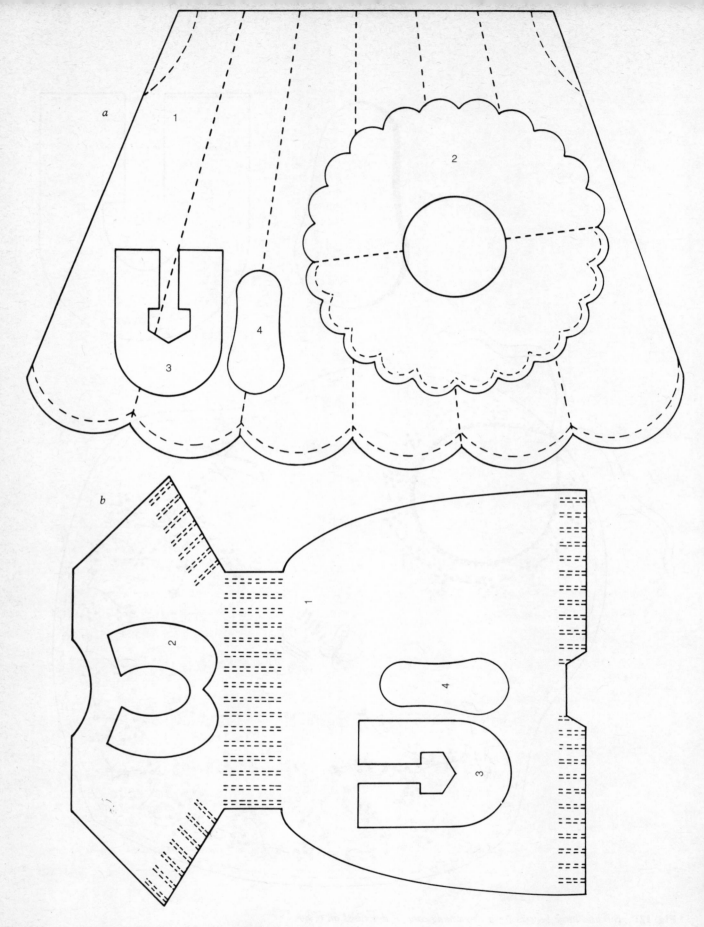

Fig. 122 *Patterns for christening cakes as described on p. 85.*

Fig. 125 *Patterns for church windows: (a) for a golden wedding anniversary (Photograph 47 on p. 127) and (b) for a Christmas or Easter cake.*

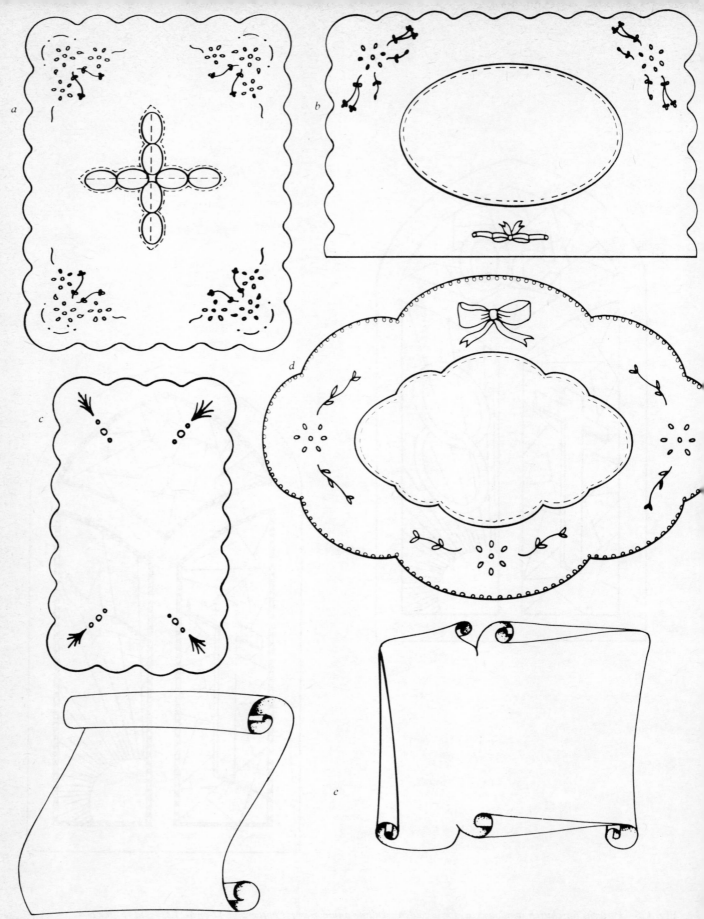

Fig. 126 *Patterns for plaques, name-cards and scrolls (Photograph 48 on p. 128) as described op pp. 87 and 88.*

Fig. 127 *Pattern 1 for cut-up cake (Photograph 20 on p. 100) as described on p. 88.*

143

230 mm

3

3

Fig. 128 *Pattern 2 for cut-up cake (Photograph 20 on p. 100) as described on p. 88.*

Fig. 130 *Patterns for the doll's clothes (Photograph 28 on p. 108) as described on p. 91.*

Fig. 131 *Pattern for bib collar (Photograph 35 on p. 115).*

Fig. 132 *Patterns for floodwork (Photograph 41 on p. 121).*

Fig. 133 *Half of the pattern for the collar on the ballerina cake made with icing used in floodwork (Photograph 43 on p. 123) as described on p. 56.*

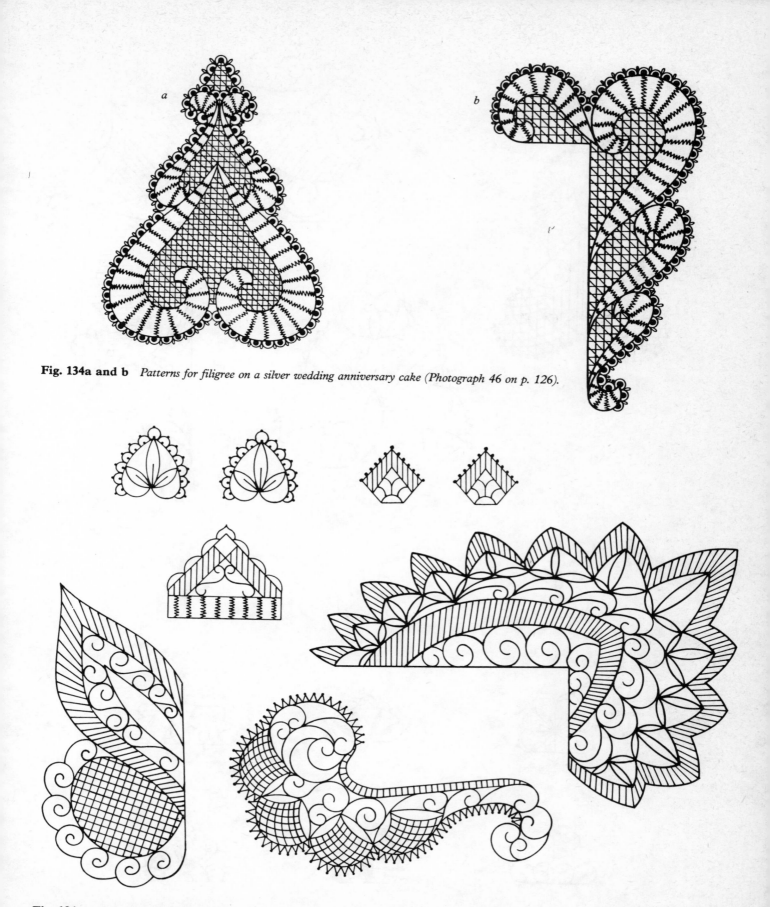

Fig. 134a and b *Patterns for filigree on a silver wedding anniversary cake (Photograph 46 on p. 126).*

Fig. 134c *More easy filigree patterns.*

Fig. 134d *More easy filigree patterns.*

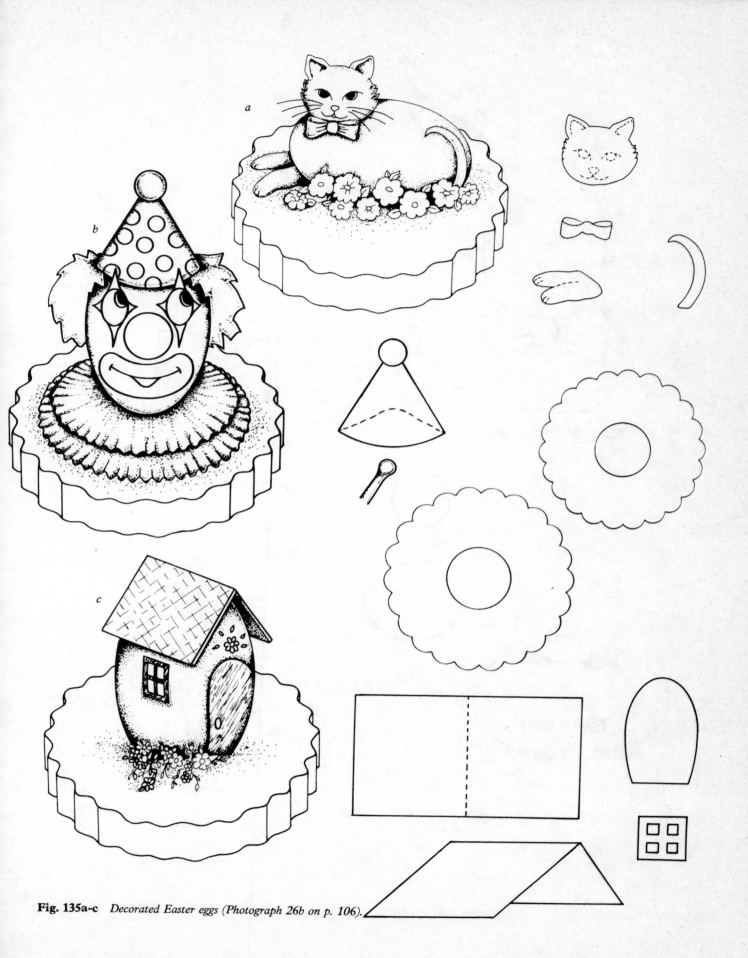

Fig. 135a-c *Decorated Easter eggs (Photograph 26b on p. 106).*

151

Fig. 135d-f *Decorated Easter eggs (Photograph 26b on p. 106).*

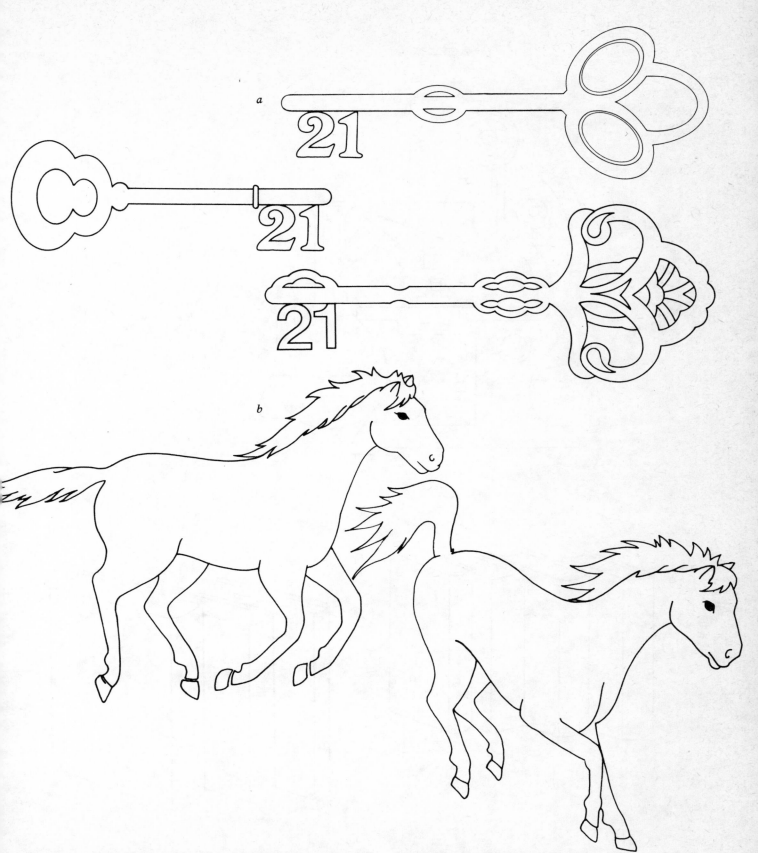

Fig. 136a and b *Patterns for a man's twenty-first birthday cake (Photograph 38 on p. 118). Fig. 136a and b can be done with icing used for floodwork, and Fig. 136b can also be used for cocoa painting on the sides of the cake.*

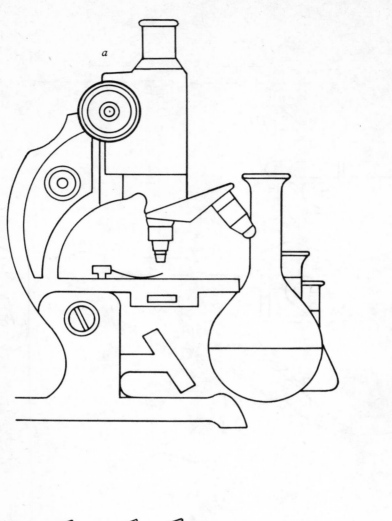

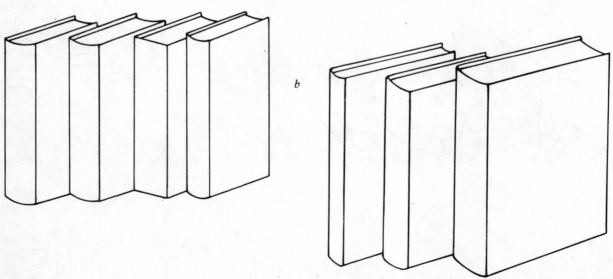

Fig. 137 *Patterns for ornaments on a man's birthday cake (Photograph 40 on p. 120) are flooded with icing used for floodwork as described on p. 92.*

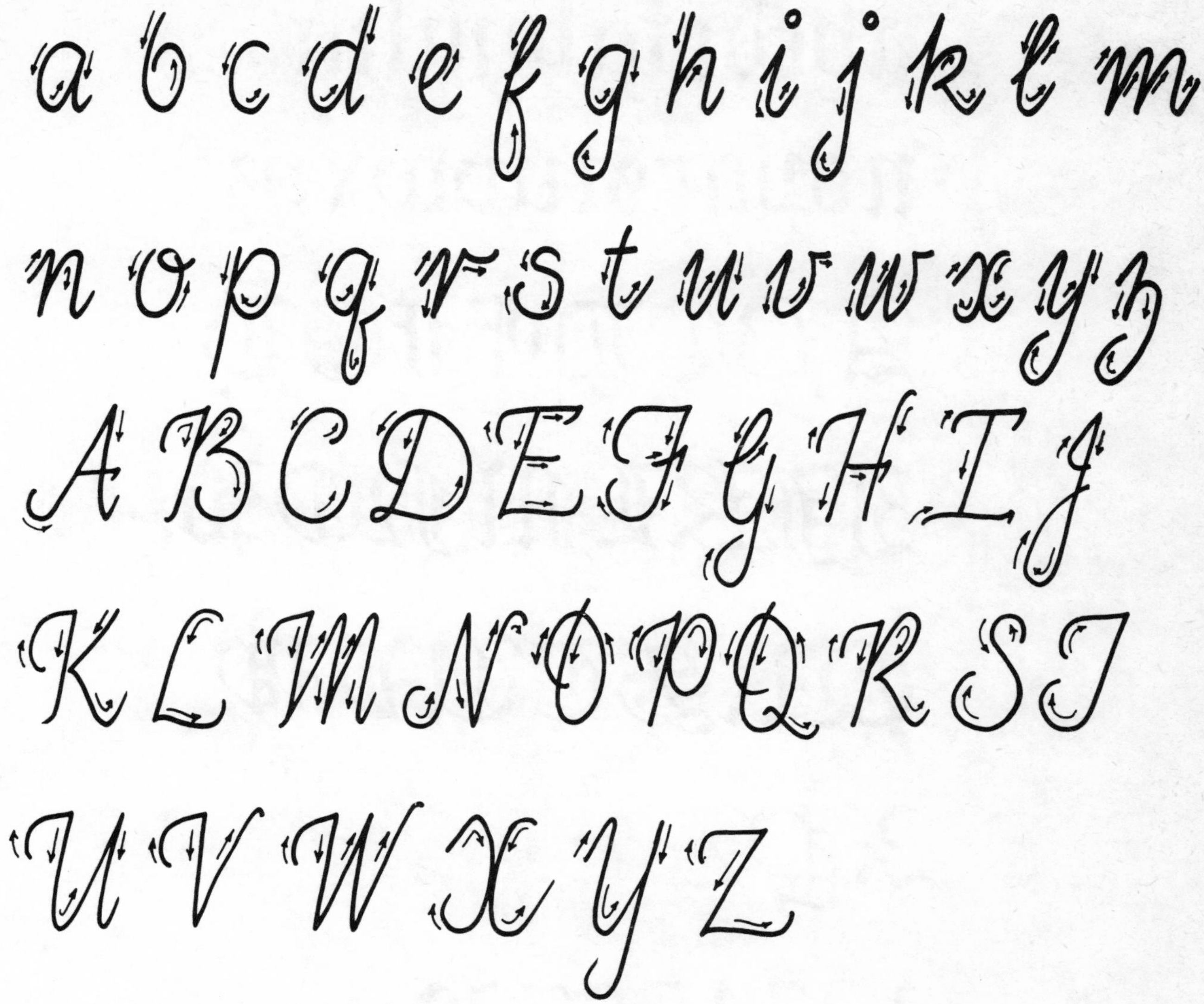

abcdefghijklm
nopqrstuvwxyz
ABCDEFGHIJ
KLMNOPQRSTJ
UVWXYZ

Fig. 138a *Examples of ornamental writing. (The arrows indicate the direction of movement.)*

abcdefghijklm

nopqrstuvwxyz

ABCDEFGH

IJKLMNOP

QRSTUVW

XYZ

1234567890

Fig. 138b *Examples of ornamental writing done with icing used for floodwork.*

Fig. 139a *Basic pattern for cakes (see Photograph 19 on p. 99) which is done in butter or royal icing.*

Fig. 139b *Pattern for a cake (Photograph 19 on p. 99).*

158

Fig. 139c *Pattern for decoration of a butter or fruitcake.*

Fig. 139d *Pattern for a basket on a butter or fruitcake.*